CONSIDER YOUR WAYS

Hamid Charles

To: My Dear Friend & Brother in Christ

From: Hamid

Prov. 3:5-6

CLM Publishing

All Scriptures quoted, unless otherwise indicated, are taken from the HOLY BIBLE, New King James Version (NKJV). Used by permission ©All rights reserved worldwide.

Contact the author Hamid Charles
IMEGE_143@LIVE.COM

Charles, Hamid

ISBN: 978-0-9971694-6-1

Published by CLM Publishing
www.shop.clmpublishing.com

Printed in the United States of America

CONTENTS

SYNOPSIS

This book is a testimony with interesting segments of my autobiography on the journey of life. If life has become a routine treadmill workout for all the wrong reasons, then this book is for you. If religion has an important part in your life, but somehow time seems to elude you, then this book is for you. If you want to know more about Jesus Christ and Christians, then this book will be very rewarding to read.

It captures some intriguing years where environmental circumstances and cultural practices were introduced to broaden my horizon into adulthood. It shares choices and benefits that have caused me to "consider my ways" in growing with patience. The desire of my heart is now to encourage others into a healthier and more meaningful relationship with the Creator.

With the help of God's Spirit, I have been able to take a probing look into the realistic behavior of my fellow beings. The art of learning will intrigue your understanding about the free gift of salvation. Remember, the proof of the pie is in the tasting. This book will offer rest to minds that are ready for answers. It will also encourage hope for all seasons of life.

It is written...........

"You shall worship the LORD your God and Him only you shall serve" (Matthew 4:10).

For the glory of God and the saints scattered across His church universal.

Beloved in Christ, chosen by the Heavenly Father is my wife, Gloria. Together we have forty years of marriage and one daughter, Melissa. She continues to build the family tree with three special grandchildren; Elianna, Ethan, and Evan are our heritage. Ian is also a pillar and a one of a kind son-in-law, all favored to us from above (1 Peter 3:5).

DEDICATION

This book is dedicated to the Penners. Reverend Bernard and his dear wife, Marguerite, served as missionaries for several years in Trinidad, West Indies.

Their godly role was manifested through the working of the Holy Spirit. It was an overwhelming labor of love among the saints which they made contact with during those years. Their journey of faith as missionaries has become a legacy dedicated to the Universal Church of Jesus Christ.

THE PENNERS

The Penners were committed missionaries who lived an exemplified lifestyle, each in ways that were unique in both character and personality. They demonstrated to the world how born-again Christians could grow in grace. That lifestyle was possible because Christ was in total control of their lives. For them it began when they both left their homelands in 1951. Bernard left his family and friends in Alberta, Canada. Marguerite left her family in Portland, Oregon. They were willing to obey God's calling to foreign mission service.

As a result of the years at Prairie Bible Institute in Three Hills, Alberta opened up windows of opportunity for both to serve. It came with challenges and vision for countries needing the gospel message. It was there they learned about the need for church missionaries in the West Indies. After receiving their doctorate degrees, they both applied through the mission board as candidates. Neither of them knew it would be the beginning of a thirty-year missionary journey. They were privileged to serve in Cuba, Jamaica, and Trinidad before retiring.

Never before did their paths cross at Prairie. To make up for financial assistance, Bernard worked in the dairy department at the college. Marguerite Schmidt fit into the musical department through singing as well as playing the piano and accordion. During the mission board process, both applications were tentatively accepted as singles. Marguerite's musical gifts indicated a definite need in Cuba with the radio ministry.

Bernard, however, was assigned to the mission in Trinidad, West Indies. It was not what he had expected. Nevertheless, with an attitude of humility, his prayer was answered. That September in 1951, Bernard had a passion to do the Lord's will when the mission board in Pennsylvania made the decision. The Lord knew the desires of his heart, and on the last day of school orientation, another prayer was answered. As the candidates were gathered, Mr. Thompson from the Trinidad mission field sent a message to Bernard.

It informed him of the need for a lady school teacher. Therefore, the Prairie Mission Board rerouted and sent him to Cuba instead. That sudden change in mission service eventually became favorable for Bernard. From then onward, the Lord worked out the details that created opportunities for them to be together doing His work. Not many months went by before they began closing the friendship gap and catching up on the miles that had separated them. One year later, on September 27, 1952, they got married in Placates, Cuba.

They continued working among the Cubans for a while before getting transferred to Trinidad. However, this new mission field meant settling down in a small fishing village. The length of time before another transfer was not on their priority list as they made home among the villagers. It was quietly seated along the Northern coast and known by the name of Sans-Souse. Their mission and labor of love sowing seeds in neighboring areas continued for eighteen years. The other districts were Blanchisseuse, La-Filette, Toco, Matalot, Arouca, Arima, Valencia, and Sangre-Grande.

Those years were filled with prayers, sweat, and tears over some challenges never anticipated. The light of the gospel began to shine in hearts that were cold and rebellious to God. Whenever the Lord calls, He eventually blossoms the faithful through bonding of relationships among the saints. The Penners became instrumental in molding newborn believers among homes and families across the Island. Some who became church pillars in their villages were the Pilgrims, Riley, Cupid, Gibson, Caraby, Christopher, and Bruce to name a few.

As their ministry began increasing, the Penners were commissioned to the Southern district of Trinidad. Their transition in 1966 came with a fresh approach to the people of Siparia. They experienced a similar hospitality and warmth from the genuine friendship among the people, especially the younger generation. Within the following two years after settling down, they introduced a camping ministry. This long-needed vision soon became a priority on the members' prayer list among fellow churches on the Island.

With no children of their own, they soon became the camp's mom and dad for many teens. Over the years, they served as directors, councilors, and other roles vital to that ministry. With such a vision, passion, and concern for the opportunity, Mr. Penner began seeking suitable property in the Northern districts. Ten years later, the Trinidad government offered a lease on suitable property near the Valencia area. However, the good news and answer to praying saints was sadly interrupted. The Prairie Mission board decided to move them to Jamaica.

They faithfully served there for three years before another mind-disturbing situation caused them to take a leave of absence. It was when Marguerite's ailing father became worse, causing them to return to Oregon. In timing with God's provincial hand, the camp committee in Trinidad requested their return. The foundational building plans for a camp facility began in 1981. Prayers were answered on Christmas Eve of 1982 when they again arrived in Trinidad. The people of the Evangelical churches in Trinidad saw the dawning of another camp facility.

This much-needed facility would be at Lily Trace in Siparia. It became "Ridge Walk Camp and Conference Center" by the grace of God. Their allegiance to Him and support from believers kept them focused during the erection of the first building. For Marguerite to leave her widowed mother alone in Portland to take her place beside her husband was an act of faith, trust, and loyalty to her husband and the Lord. This appeared to be the biggest challenge they were about to face.

It was also the continuation of a relationship for me and other believers at Siparia Evangelical Church. They periodically preached and taught at church during the construction years of the camp. Their ministry was also an encouragement to believers in the outer districts of Morne-Diablo, Quinam, and Penal. Prior to that camping ministry, the Penners became instrumental in church planting in those areas. From her home in Portland, Oregon came a few lines from Mrs. Penner's selection from an old hymn.

With mercy and with judgment, my web of time He wove, and aye the dews of sorrow were clustered with His love, I'll bless the hand that guided, I'll bless the heart that planned, when throned where glory dwelled in Immanuel's land.

Because of circumstances beyond their control concerning family matters in Portland, Mrs. Penner had to leave earlier than expected. Shortly after, Bernard closed shop and joined his beloved wife in Portland. With God's blessing, many eyes dripped as we waved them farewell.

Mrs. Penner left in May 1991, and Mr. Penner left in August of the same year. Both left with a sense of accomplishment in fulfilling the Lord's will at the camp. It is to these two extraordinary God-fearing people I'm dedicating this book, *Consider Your Ways*. I desire for each person who reads it to become a better steward of God's grace. May we all learn how effective our lives can be to those looking for godly role models. Walk the talk as the Lord expects each of His children to do. Mr. Penner went home from Portland, Oregon to be with His Lord and Savior in May 2007.

INTRODUCTION

As a new believer in Christ, it took me a long time to realize that there is no neutral ground in the Christian faith. Growing stronger in the faith does not depend on speed, age, agility, wealth, or earthly favoritism. What I have found over the years that matters in experiencing the joy of my salvation is discipline and accountability to my Lord. My reason for spilling so much ink over these pages is for both saved and unsaved readers to catch a glimpse of the reality of Christianity.

The hope is for all to *"consider your ways"* and experience the effectiveness of the Holy Spirit's guidance. The forging of this new lifestyle can penetrate amidst the everyday norms. Regardless of circumstances, help from the Creator God is available for all. This is only possible when Christ has become the author and finisher of such a life. Although obstacles continue to manifest themselves in rows of pain and death, Heaven's eternity gives way for the redemption of saints.

This is a journey with Christ that allows me to recognize my potential and limitations. It strengthens my imperfection regarding physical and spiritual challenges. At the same time, I know that in Christ all my inadequacy can be fulfilled according to His purpose. This verse changes my mental equilibrium when I'm caught below the barrel, trying to reach upward.

He encourages his followers to *"[t]rust in Him with all our heart and lean not to our own understanding, in all our ways acknowledge Him, then He will direct our path"* (Prov. 3:5-6 with emphasis). Although this new identity does not automatically erase my sinful human nature, it does in many ways provide graceful leverage for me to be *"pressing forward towards the goal for the prize of the upward call of God in Christ Jesus"* (Phil. 3:14). Therefore, my friend, do not be anxious to erect walls of defensive conclusions.

Nor entertain unsuitable thoughts that often prevent the mind from handling the truth. The gospel message has become my story. As a result, changes have occurred because *"greater is He that is in me, than He that is in the world"* (1 Jn. 4:4). One of several lessons I'm learning as age increases, is that of paying attention to how well I must run this race. The writer of Hebrews encourages the Christians to *"lay aside every weight and the sin which so easily ensnares us, so that we may run with endurance"* (Heb. 12:1).

I heartily say thank you to all my faithful and dedicated friends. You have graciously assisted with a spirit of love and dedication. As a result, I hope to share a clearer view of my thoughts and the intentions this book offers. May the Lord of Glory receive all the praise and honor as we all consider our ways (Hag. 1:5-7). With godly tutelage and in company of maturing saints, my prayer is to weave a tapestry of hope for curious minds so it will germinate hunger for the living word of God. That is why I often consider my life to be a book.

Be it small or large, its title or preface, I will begin with conversion. Remember, it is a work in progress that has taken years, months, weeks, and days. Therefore, each page, chapter and line will have history written for all eternity. Therefore, I must attend to transparency for the inspection of my enemies as well as friends. Every word, thought, and gesture is under the eye of God. I have to do it reverently, without levity, yet without constraint or terror. This will be read before His Majesty, the King of Glory, so I must write each line well.

Chapter one begins with some background history in context to the introduction. This overview allows me to transport you to the feet of Christ where He is delivering a sermon. Out of many parables comes this unique statement in Matthew 7:13. I believe it is synonymous with the kingdom of Heaven. Jesus' teaching identifies with the role model that believers should emulate. As a Leader, He became a servant. As a servant, He obeyed His Heavenly Father.

Chapter two brings a fresh visage of challenges with hope that is possible for all believers. Understanding John 14:6 provides adequate strength for every day's journey. Sometimes my mind struggles with submissiveness when my heart wants obedience. Only through the help of the Holy Spirit will I be able to experience the peace that passes all understanding. This is something man is not capable of achieving by himself. As a result, humanity is heading for destruction.

Chapter three reminds me that all is not lost, even if circumstances change. Keeping company with wrong persons eventually comes with a high price. God's wisdom, echoed through King Solomon, is found in Proverbs 22:6. This instruction is applicable for all parents, guardians, and those experiencing difficulty in grooming children. It comes with great earthly benefits and eternal rewards. It is the key to a successful society.

Chapter four elaborates upon the apostle's instructions to young Timothy from 2 Tim. 3:16. It focuses on our present objectives with three basic elements. These we find contextually preserved in the annals of time. They come with grave concerns from the very heartbeat of the author. They have the ability to affect the mental, physical, and spiritual stages of growth in lives that are committed to righteousness.

Chapter five takes us to a scene where Jesus is addressing a crowd. It is similar to most conservative congregations today. He shares wisdom in Matt. 13:30 that is not readily accepted. This is where the "rubber meets the road." Doctrine before duty then comes precept before practice. It takes hard work to develop, but then again, we are followers in the Lord's army.

Chapter six introduces Romans 12:1b with a refreshing spirit for Christians whose hearts are submissive. The reflection of Jesus is emulated through His disciples, especially His earthly brother, James. They witnessed this truth while walking together along the dusty roads from Galilee to Jerusalem. Years after His ascension, each disciple gained a heart that knew what it meant to *"present his body as a living sacrifice."*

Let us journey that path and observe culture and politics rubbing shoulders with religion as ancient history unfolds. Let's follow the footprints of the Son of God.

Chapter seven deals with the prophet Jeremiah in chapter 29:11. It continues to remind us about the greatest news worth sharing. He pens the spoken thoughts of the Lord. *"For I know the thoughts that I think towards you, says the Lord thoughts of peace and not of evil, to give you a future and a hope."* All of that in the world will pass away. Wealth, fame, prestige, and self-glory will end with death. This new-dwelling place is with Christ.

Chapter One

IT CAME TO PASS

One particular phrase is often taken for granted, yet it hinges on history and time. These are the words "and it came to pass." Without which, the further fulfillment of scripture would be incomplete. They are used in Old Testament prophecies to seal its validation. Without them, further revelations would be void. These five simple words give glory to the Majestic God. The authority of the triune God is full of assurance. They come with faith and hope for the people of God. Regardless of any generation within the geographical locations of society, scripture will come to pass.

The prophet Isaiah wrote, "*So shall My words be that goeth out of my mouth; it shall not return unto Me void, but it shall accomplish that which I please, and it shall come to prosper in the things whereto I sent it*" (Isa. 55:11). Thanks be to our Creator for allowing only human beings to share in the "knowledge and power" of verbalizing. Perhaps it is why we should be so mindful of how we use words. Unthinkable is the saying "*sticks and stones may break my bones but words can't.*"

Yet, grave wounds that have lasted a lifetime have evolved from spilling tongues. It is why I have to be mindful of my words and the meditation of my heart. Regardless of the fluency and myriads of literacy I may acquire, words have the power to bring about freedom. Words also convey the haunting notes of guilt and condemnation. They possess healing and forgiveness.

Words of compassion can remove despair and replace them with hope to ears near and far. Therefore, with these assurances, allow me the opportunity to begin my intriguing journey. Again is coming with selected moments from days, months, and years. They are wrapped in bundles of reality and held together by the grace of God. From the cradle to footsteps of maturity is the fleeting years of my story. However, it will be selective so as to set apart the fine prints of scrutiny for my autobiography. It will be a sequential drama in which I hope to become a blessing amidst confessions.

I hope its pages will attract reasoning and also share pleasurable moments of challenges for each reader. My delightful surprises are to encourage curious hearts and eager minds that are restless. My blessing comes with conditions, and my failure also comes with a price. However, the Lord often creates avenues to enjoy rainbows, even if they appear between the sunshine and rainy days of life. When King David acknowledged the depravity of his heart before the High and Lofty God, he said, *"Behold, I was shapen in iniquity; in sin did my mother conceive me"* (Ps. 51:5).

I believe my destiny has already been forecast by God's grace. Therefore, by faith, I hope to reach that divine climax. It is beyond the golden horizon where justice prevails. The Lord Jesus shared an illustration regarding the journey of life. He referred to two destinations, and each person has the free will to choose. One is named *"the broad road"* which has become very popular and loved by many. The first couple of pilgrims who forged this broad road refused to heed the warning.

Therefore, they were sent out from the splendors of Heaven that were reflected in the Garden of Eden. Since that road was opened, mankind has no desire of turning back. God said that road *"leads to destruction"* (Matt. 7:13b). However, in mercy, another road has been provided. It is not attractive at a glance. It appears to be difficult with uncomfortable challenges. It is called *"the narrow way."* This challenging terrain takes us back to that final destination. Whoever chooses this way will experience the refreshing green pastures of life. This way guarantees safety amidst the valley of the shadow of death.

I have found serenity and contentment during dull moments along this adventurous path. This is the path which *"leads to life everlasting."* There are no shortcuts that will bring anyone to this path. Although God knew the depth of my heart was filled with hostility and inconceivable actions against Him, He graciously provided me (and all mankind) with this alternative way. No one has to continue on that broad road to destruction. Opportunities always come when a person realizes that life entails more than just existing.

2

Divine help is the only means of getting on that "narrow way." It will require faith found only in the person of Jesus Christ (Heb. 12:2a). Only through God's grace I can testify (with millions around the world) who have been snatched from the broad road and placed on the way *"that leads to life everlasting."* This transformation is possible because of the crossroads between Gethsemane and Golgotha. It became a destination from Heaven to Hell and back.

So then, I will share a few chapters from my journal of life along the *"broad road."* Then by the grace of God I will continue with new experiences on the *"narrow way."* It commences from humble beginnings in the district of Siparia. This village was established in 1758 by the Capuchin priests from Aragon, Spain. It is located in the county of Saint Patrick as part of the land of the Hummingbird. However, it was named La Isla de la Trinidad by Christopher Columbus upon rediscovering it in August 1498. From then until now, it has become the melting pot for a diversity of ethnic cultures.

Streaming from all walks of life, each nation has contributed to building her into a jewel of the Caribbean. Trinidad is now home to over one million residents. It has become the envy of many nations with a colorful assortment of traditions. With strong financial and economic growth, it has become a leader among nations. She has elevated herself from the grass roots of colonialism to the footsteps of independence. In recent years, Trinidad has been recognized on the platform of world trading as a Twin Island Republic Nation.

Siparia is located in the Southern part of that island. It has a rich heritage of earthen minerals and agricultural produce. Religious activities are celebrated annually and attract citizens on both islands. One in particular is the street procession in homage of the patron saint of the Capuchin missions.

The church of La Divina Pastora officially became a Roman Catholic parish in 1906. The feast day of La Divina Pastora as well as "Siparia Fete" occurs on the second Sunday after Easter (Excerpt from TriniView.com).

That second Sunday morning after Easter, hundreds of worshipers join in celebration at the cathedral on Mary Street. Part of the church

3

agenda for that occasion is to organize a procession along designated streets encompassing the church building. The chanting of the Holy Mary Mother of God prayer is repeatedly echoed among the thousands making the walk. It's a weekend that also attracts athletes to perform on the cycling arena. Gamblers with their makeshift tents and game boards are situated on the sidewalks adjacent to High Street.

It is a carnival-type of atmosphere with merry-go-rounds and chair-plane rides on the outer perimeter of Irvin Park Savannah. Each attraction has its enticing moments to passersby. Small sections along the back streets are marked and sold by the County Council. These ten by six feet vendor spaces are transformed into huts for overnighting. Some begin before sunrise on Saturday in preparation to sell raw and cooked food until late Saturday night. You can find a variety of local dishes with homemade candies and pastries.

Not forgetting the fresh seasonal fruits to awaken the appetite of the meddling crowd for the weekend celebration. Other religious denominations in the community also have their annual events with similar fashions. These activities make Siparia an attractive district to live in or visit. It has that compelling atmosphere which attracts a charismatic crowd. However, the fleeting years have brought a transition in leadership that has adapted fresh thinkers. Nevertheless, amidst these changes, home will always have sentimental memories.

Few but noticeable are the aged faces which continue to greet visiting residents like my wife and me. We also get the privilege to celebrate with those whose dreams have now come to pass. People and places have been transformed since we waved goodbye three decades ago. Changes good and indifferent have sifted the hearts of family priorities. Progress like a revolving wheel, brings with her changes. Sometimes the cost can be higher than expected. Nevertheless, God is merciful to allow us a shift in position by reorganizing our destiny.

The stories of the old streets of Siparia will always transport my heart to days of reminiscing. The old environment has been rebirthed with modern engraining. The eager contractors have removed boundaries from hilltops and valleys to create a level playing field. Places where no one once dared to dwell during my roaming years have become home for many. Gone are the green fields of adventure and hunting. God built the country, and now it is being replaced with man's city of cement and steel. The new influx has only to rely on the older caretakers for tales of country living.

As a young boy I enjoyed listening to raindrops beating upon zinc sheets on the roof of our house. It had that hypnotizing sound at bedtime. Today it has been substituted with the hum of an air-conditioning motor. Living abroad after 16 years of marriage in Trinidad, we are privileged to visit other destinations more frequently (when cash-flow permits). The shift in economics has allowed some of my childhood dreams to come to pass.

Visiting other Caribbean islands, I have noticed similar family infrastructure. Their cultural practices are familiar to those of Trinidad. On their street markets they sell seasonal vegetation locally grown along with arts and crafts. Animals are slaughtered and sold on special occasions to maintain a fresh supply. Each of these Caribbean islands comes with their unique geographical wonder. This has allowed natives and tourists the opportunity to experience the serene beauty of God's creation. Perhaps the early migration of immigrants was partly responsible for the similarity of environmental surroundings. Their country houses are fashioned with intriguing artistic structuring noticeable even today in some places.

I thank the Lord for such memories which I hope to pass on to my grandchildren. From the echoes of our modern Christian families comes an appeal for peace and contentment. Daily prayers are ongoing for political and religious leaders who are being taken in by greed and power. Our younger generation is witnessing the prophecies of their parents coming to pass. Some who are entrusted with authority display a sense of disregard and lack of ambition, to build a safer community. I ponder the thought of their spiritual education, as some of the early ancestors were explorers of the Bible. The wise living from the less fortunate who were a bit gullible in regards to biblical knowledge.

Nevertheless, God is merciful with divine grace. Could it be that they were not necessarily gospel evangelists? It was once echoed in homes that *"charity begins at home, and do unto others as you would have them do unto you."* Sadly today there are so many homes being replaced for houses. This happens when family members live like tenants. Immature parents are expecting teachers and institute instructors to repair our broken communities. The full arm of the law can often be obstructed due to privileges or unjust favors.

However, God's mercy, grace, and love will be justly awarded to all without favoritism. All of His privileges infringe on Biblical principles. They benefit our agendas if only we allow him the privilege. I live in a society where many children are unsupervised. They have nothing to do and plenty of time to do it. As a teen, one of my false assumptions was to believe that the grass on the other side of the fence was much greener. Add years of maturity to that thought, and the story about the dog and the bone comes to mind.

In my primary school reading book was an interesting story about a dog. The dog had a bone in his mouth and saw his reflection in a pond. He instantly let go of the bone to go after the one that appeared to be bigger the water. In silent contemplation, the God of accountability says to me *"so are the ways of everyone who is greedy for gain; it takes away the life of its owners"* (Prov. 1:19). I have also found as much pleasurable taste for spiritual development when obedience is cultivated. The steadfast words of Christ require all followers *"to walk by faith"* (2 Cor. 5:7). What we see may not necessarily be what we thought it to be.

The comforts of life for me as a believer vary with age. At the tender age of four attending pre-school, it seemed comfortable to be disobedient. Today I have learned never to assume "sinning" was less effective in the early stages of life as it is today. The good old days, as some say, came with challenges and bitter moments of regret. I did not anticipate the change spiritual knowledge would bring as the years passed. I am thankful to Ms. Jackeline's preschool. It was there I was introduced to a spiritual foundation for life.

The preschool was located on Mary Street within a short walking distance from our home. Class was held within an enclosed area of the "dancing floor" upstairs. This large two-story wooden building served as the community center to accommodate approximately three hundred persons. On weekends and special occasions, it was transformed into an arena for indoor sports and celebrations. There were no governmental prerequisites for any ambitious person to open a preschool. It was also an opportunity to gain employment for some.

Therefore, those who operated such an establishment were generally affiliated with some religious denomination. Ms. Jackeline lived two blocks away from our home. It was convenient to collect and drop me on her way to school whenever my older siblings were preoccupied. She was a dedicated Roman Catholic imparting knowledge from the Bible. There were other religious denominations catering to younger children within close proximity to our home. Ms. Jackeline's character and popularity won the hearts of my mom and siblings.

Then, in time, the "seed" was sown and the Lord brought the increased. He sent missionaries to water and groom my faith in Christ. This would be when the first Evangelical church was established in Siparia with foreign missionaries. However, church planting in other Northern districts had already begun; their head office was in the district of Arima. The Christian doctrine was already proselytized by the Capuchin priests from Spain in 1758. Then, over the centuries, came the Hindus, Muslims, and other Christian denominations planting their roots.

In the late 1950s, the villagers in Siparia welcomed the Peters family. Their mission was evangelism by visiting homes in the neighborhood. After came the ingathering at their home for worship. This eventually blossomed into a church format with a Sunday school for young people from 4 pm - 5 pm. These gatherings caught the attention of sinners who were hungry for the "Living Word." My inquisitive mind was intrigued with the flannel board bible stories. The missionaries also did puppetry and paper art. With Easter and Christmas concerts we were taught new choruses that made us feel honored on stage.

There was something new and more interesting to gossip about in Siparia. Attendees were reflecting friendliness in ways never before practiced in other religious gatherings. Nevertheless, my mother and I attended morning worship at the Open Bible church in San Fernando. It was adjacent to the Public Bus Transport Corporation, which was convenient for us. My timidity was eventually overcome by the time I stepped into late teens. Then with new acquaintances at this new Evangelical church, I began learning that the world does not revolve around me.

My Father never felt the desire to attend many religious functions. However, as a boy, he did attend a catholic church. He was a loner who kept himself occupied with work. This included repairs and maintenance on his vehicles. My older brothers got involved with automotive repairs by assisting him. We all became familiar with tools and various trades handed down from him and our grandfather. Perhaps it is why being an auto mechanic became a career for me.

His foresight and wisdom will always be remembered as I continue to share it with the younger generations of my family. To God be the glory for placing me under his supervision. Although, at that foolish age, I thought he never loved me nor was concerned about my future. How wrong I was to judge when I look back and see how it came to pass. I realize my younger years were nothing short of a miracle. I've witnessed the hand of the Lord rearranging circumstances so that I was blessed. He received the glory as I began to succeed in this vocation.

Although He has interrupted lives of loved ones through death, I can say the things I've learned have also been a blessing to others along my journey in life. God's blessing should lead all to His free gift, salvation. This is an opportunity to share my carousel life full of radical flavors. It is enriched with victories and defeats on that narrow road to a wonderful future. It is a promise He has prepared for all who will love and serve Him. I urge you now to "consider your ways" before time slips away. Remembering more at age ten has helped me put things into perspective.

This was the report whispered among my older siblings, as I thoroughly took advantage of my position. I was a spoiled, miserable, cry-cry baby, and yet loved by all for seven years until the arrival of another baby sister. With this interruption, the family attention was shifted to her. However, this lasted for a short while until the arrival of another baby girl. She completed the family circle of nine. From where I was standing, life seemed to be slipping by very quickly. Mom was confined to babysitting in the ministry of home affairs.

Nevertheless, it was during those developing years as a teenager, I continued to learn more about my family. I found out about our very own skeletons in the closet. Then, as knowledge increased, so did my curiosity. But *"wisdom is found on the lips of him who has understanding"* (Prov. 10:13). I also realized that with much knowledge, comes greater responsibility. I was not about to search among dead bones for new life. Therefore, my journey continued to unveil with a deeper passion for weightlifting during the youthful years of strength and vitality.

This disciplined sport prompted an athletic life despite my motives. Not long before that, with a frail physique, I graduated from primary school. At twelve years old, it was the time to consider two options. Firstly, to seek the labor market for whatever was available. Secondly, I could return to an educational institute. Making the decision involved many sleepless nights. The idea of having nothing to do (jobless) and plenty of time to do it was frightful. Thank the Lord my parents, especially my dad who began to enlighten me about responsibilities around the home.

My Mom also gave instructions in housekeeping, which became part of my daily chores. There were chores that included painting, masonry, plumbing, mechanics, and other activities that kept me occupied. Every Saturday morning the yard, which included beneath the house and outer surroundings, had to be cleaned. It meant sweeping and burning dry tree leaves, pulling weeds, and emptying garbage. My two older brothers toted water from a standpipe for my mother to do the weekly laundering by hand.

They also took turns chopping logs to make fire sticks for our local dirt stove. With these responsibilities soon to inherit when they left home, I saw no plans or future desire to become a "somebody" whenever adult life arrived. Those empty, vague thoughts were my first set of stepping stones on the road to reality. It shadowed a frightful forecast outside the plans of the Lord. I recall wishing for life's pleasures and whatever else was out there to attract this new kid on the block. Regrettably, on some Saturdays, my chores took priority over football and cricket with friends in the village.

However, I enjoyed volleyball and other activities at the church. The Friday youth meetings made up for lost opportunities during the week. Whenever possible on weekends, I joined forces with several boys to go cycling. It was challenging to ride fifteen miles to Quanim Beach and back in less than thirty minutes. Growing into manhood from the school of hard knocks with sweat and tears have paid off for me today. With my dad and my brothers as teachers, they kept me focused.

Often *"in my distress I cried unto the Lord, and he heard me, I poured out my complaint before him"* (Ps. 120:1 & Ps. 142:2a). It took some years before the Lord adjusted my work attitude. He also knew how to change the circumstances surrounding my complaints. I eventually found out that during difficult times, my prayer life was more regular and sincere. Therefore, praying for patience made me learn how to be more content. As age increased, so did other opportunities that caught my attention.

Occasionally, on public holidays, some of the older teens who attended church would organize a lime[1] on the beach. We used the public bus for transportation since no one owned a vehicle. This and similar outdoor activities always fostered healthy relationships. One of several lessons was learning to accept others as we grew to maturity in Christ. Interacting also provided the opportunity to hear, see, and learn in relationships among single individuals who later got married. The church was the best place for me to find a partner for life.

Without realizing, my interest for the movies began to sidetrack me from attending church. I was replacing the Sunday evening services for the cinema. The manager and operators (as it appeared to me) cunningly selected religious and historical Bible-based films. I thought it was to draw the religious crowd (like myself) on Sunday evenings. Therefore, I patiently made the effort to attend by saving my extra pocket change. This included the earnings from my grandfather and mom during the week.

On some Saturday mornings, my grandfather took my brothers and me with him to his seven-acre plantation. It was about five miles away from home. We enjoyed ripe bananas, oranges, sugar cane,

---

[1] Liming is a Trinidadian street dialect commonly used to express an open free time slot. It creates a temporary escape from the norm of responsibilities to engage in personal satisfaction with other companies.

mangoes, plums and cherries, to name a few, after reaping the cocoa and coffee crops. Then we loaded all into the truck and sat at the back, resting as he drove very slowly home. Upon arrival we had to off load and divide the produce. We got yams, cassava, green bananas, and other produce to take home for our mother.

My grandfather was never anxious to give monetary gifts for our labor. Nevertheless, he gave back what we sowed as our reward. Therefore, trying to convince him for twenty-five cents took a lot of spit and patience. During those wearisome minutes of waiting, the Lord kept reminding me that patience is a virtue not bought with silver or gold. My grandfather never had a bank account as a proprietor and landlord. Therefore, all his valuables were kept in his bedroom chest.

His later years were spent on his reclining chair in the gallery. His grandchildren and great-grandchildren would visit him in the evening to listen to stories he encountered during his life. My race to the cinema was always tiresome, but rewarding. Watching stories from the Bible with characters like Moses, Abraham, and David created a desire to continue attending the cinema. However, I always went back to my Bible to check the facts. With the truth, I was able to recognize where and what the film producers added and subtracted from the original stories. Visual aids helped me unfold biblical history that has come to pass.

One of which was the Exodus account of the Hebrew people. It was led by one man who felt it was impossible, yet obeyed through divine intervention. History now records the rebirth of this nation, from which the whole world has benefited. Although their journey was dangerous and seems unrealistic, it came to pass. We're told they grumbled, complained, and became ungrateful, yet out of many came one. A forty-year designated journey to a Promised Land did come to pass; similarly my grandfather's stories came to pass.

My senior years as a believer in Jesus Christ bear record that what has happened in my past and what is yet to come is no coincidence. Another remarkable adventure in history was with Abraham. He was also instructed to leave his family and comfort zone to walk thousands of miles without a map or compass. He had no global positioning system, only faith and obedience that eventually led him to an inheritance for future generations. Without history, the evidence of my Christian faith becomes a myth.

It would be similar to exist without a conscience. I would become unaccountable if there was no "built in" guidance system from my Creator. His hand-formed creatures were designed with the capacity to identify truth from error. However, when "man" was separated, the "Holy" aspect of that divine relationship was broken. No longer were the Creator and the creature able to meet face-to-face as was in the garden. It became the reason that has caused skeptics to boast in ignorance about the Triune Holy God.

Therefore, as a rule of thumb, all rebellious hearts deny the incarnation of Jesus Christ, but believe in a god. Even in His earthly appeals, Jesus Christ journeyed to the cross with love for skeptics. Sunday school and youth meetings increased my hunger to learn about that man from Galilee. Then, when I was older and attending Bible Study and prayer meetings, the Lord began testing my faith. The lust of my eyes began desiring the glowing things I wanted to possess. During such battles between the Spirit of God and my heart, I was reminded of Luke 16:13: "*You cannot serve God and mammon.*" It was a struggle whenever I put duty before doctrine. One foolish thought is to believe the Lord would understand my temporary cravings and allow me the pleasures of sin for a season (Heb. 11:25b). In God's sight, my actions were not louder than my thoughts. Even in times of envying the lifestyle of the ungodly, His word reminded me of my allegiances to Him. On one occasion at the cinema, I was confronted with my faithfulness to the church and the Lord.

The famous movie by Cecil B.D. Mills awoke my heart. I became very emotional when Moses (portrayed by Charlton Heston) was driven out of Egypt by the stubborn-hearted Pharaoh (portrayed by Yule Brynner) in the Ten Commandments. Sitting on the same bench among older men, I began crying. One turned and said to me, "*You should not be here.*" In the following days, those words sparked a breath of reality. I began to ponder about the Lord returning for His church (2 Pet. 3:10). If it were to happen while I was at the cinema, I'd be left behind.

Bear with me. At this point in my spiritual growth, I was doctrinally ignorant. I also realized that Bible-based movies always met the desires of the religious public. Since this became a stumbling block in my path, the will had to remove that desire. By God's grace, I stopped attending the cinema. It was a habit that was costly and time consuming. For replacement, when my finances could not support it, I went walking along the country roads enjoying the scenery. Sometimes I went "liming" with friends to maintain the bridge of communication.

I realized that the cinema was entertaining and educational, but it was affecting my spiritual growth. As I grew older in this habit, regular fellowship with the saints became more challenging. Although salvation is a free gift, I began to realize how costly it would be for the rest of my natural life. I am living in a world where Jesus Christ is not welcome in many homes.

To remain at home without a permanent job was frustrating. Those years brought a doubting faith that caused a double minded heart to the finished work on the Cross. Not until age sixteen did the Lord begin providing temporary jobs. One was with the borough of Saint Patrick County Council. During the months of June to August, the availability of pipe-borne water became limited to certain districts. Contractors bid for employment with the borough council.

Trucks equipped with 800 and 1200 gallon water tanks were designated to those districts. Each contractor's vehicle was assigned with a "water checker" employed by the county. The job was to record and distribute each load of water. This helped pay bills at home and provided pocket change for personal spending. It also provided opportunities to share the gospel with unsaved friends. Most conversations evolved whenever "religion" became the day's topic. Some, for the joy of ignorance, made fun of Christ and His followers.

Others prided themselves by using scripture out of context to defend their personal habits and gains. Those types of dialogues happened mostly under the influence of alcohol. Nevertheless, the Lord continued to favor me at various intervals with neighborhood jobs. Identifying who I was in Christ and what my doctrine taught were my opening remarks to new acquaintances. I heard several schools of thoughts on religion, but only the Christian faith brings its promises to pass. For some folks *"promises are like babies; easy to make, but hard to deliver"* (Pastor Josh Manly).

Only by God's grace was I learning to accept ridicule and testing from those who had yet to experience the joy of His salvation. With the maturing of years, it was time to catch up on brighter years of courage and boldness. Although there were some filled with foolish decisions, my desire was to seek out the good God had blessed me with. Regrettably, there was a period of backsliding from the fellowship. I felt the desires of the world to be more interesting. This occurred during the short period when my older siblings and their children discontinued their attendance.

My two younger sisters would occasionally attend, but they never saw the need to get serious with the Lord. I allowed myself to slip into a dried season. This often happens to believers who are left to wander without the watchful eyes of shepherds. Although I was in church, church was not in me. I had all the formality but had not yet grown to appreciate who I was in Christ. I had yet to learn about His purpose for saving me. The Lord continued working on me during the summer camps and carnival weekend retreats.

I began to get closer in relationship to Him through small group devotions and discussions, thanks to dedicated counselors whose programs were designed to attract young people to the Lord. Gospel-centered retreats often have this effect on all attendees. I can testify on how helpful they have been to me. Therefore, my interest for others who were not able to attend was to focus on a similar facility in the southern district of Trinidad. If this visionary dream came to pass, the influence of a gospel-centered lifestyle would reach all ages in the surrounding villages of Siparia.

Building and operating such a facility was the vision of Reverend Bernard Penner. Many years later, it has come to pass, accommodating people of all ages. Since its inception, it has drawn many congregations of evangelical churches closer together. However, my journey at that time seemed stagnant without a regular flow of income. I ignorantly conceived that the Lord did not seem to understand my problems. My major concern was what would happen when my older brothers left home. What would my life be without a secure job?

At the present I was grateful to be earning 18 TT dollars as a pump attendant at Ahamad's Gas Station in Santa Flora. Although it was not a dream come true, each week it provided bus fare, lunch, and dinner snacks, and ten dollars allowance for my mom. Unlike my brother-in-law who was the General Manager of the station, I was eighteen and lacked a qualification. Returning to the classroom to further my education was an option I did not want to consider. Nevertheless, by the grace of God, it did come to pass.

In the meantime, when I considered my financial responsibilities as the last son living at home, securing a permanent job was my first priority. I made the best of each day's work whenever it came my way. I continued attending church and hoped my prayer request for a permanent job would someday come to pass.

My fond memories of the first family arriving from Canada as missionaries had a lasting impact on my life as a young boy. They were sent and supported by the World Team Mission in collaboration with the Reverend Dr. Billy Graham Evangelistic Association. Reverend Harold Peters, his wife Hazel and their three children became an outstanding family in our community. Rodney, Beverly, and Dickey fitted into our environment like cold butter on hot bread. It was not long before they began learning to adapt to our ethnic culture and neighborhood practices. They were different in personalities, but it did not create boundaries among the children who attended church. Children who have a God-fearing environment grow healthier.

Jesus often references children during His ministry: *"We should borrow that unstinting trust of a child in its parents for dealing with each other"* (Queen Elizabeth 11). Today, by God's grace, I am trying to reflect a similar role model to my nine-year-old granddaughter and two grandsons. Their pleasant smiles and gentle words of greeting transcend cultures and nationalities. I believe children have the ability to blend in more quickly than adults; adults prefer to be more cautious and keep their distance.

I found it excusable at times to allow my instincts to rule my heart, instead of allowing love to reign (1 Cor. 10:24). That type of transition into sainthood comes with growing pains over many years if the Lord permits. Nevertheless, the Lord was enabling me to grow by stretching my personality beyond those shy stages of childhood. Jesus knew how effectively verbal communication would assist us. He knew how our emotions and reasoning could be expressed to build healthy relationships. Adam did exactly this when he saw Eve and recited the first poem to her (Gen. 2:23).

This phenomenal attribute was not intended for the animal kingdom. Except for ministering angels, man is allowed the opportunity to proclaim the good news of Salvation. King Solomon reminded his son to *"pay attention to his wisdom, and lend an ear to his understanding so that he may preserve discretion."* (Prov. 5:1-2 with emphasis). Because I want to be a godly role model, my humility and attitude will take a lifetime of discipline from the Lord (Matt. 18:2-5). The Peters shared their lives with the Siparia community.

Strangers saw the transparency of the gospel as they went on a door-to-door crusade in the neighborhood. It was their act of faithfulness which brought an increase to the worship gatherings. The first introduction to Sunday school started beneath the Peters rented house. It started at four in the afternoon and was over by 5 pm. Then, Bible study and prayer on Wednesday nights, and a youth meeting eventually started on Saturday evenings from 5 pm to 7 pm. The news about an evangelistic church began to spread like wildfire as folks from surrounding districts attended.

Some as far as five miles away came walking in search of the "Living Word." The simplicity of expositions from the Bible and its interesting lessons were more appealing compared to those I recalled at my primary school devotions. I was fortunate to attend a "Presbyterian" mission school. Bible teaching was part of the school curriculum; however, the exposition was not as clear or meaningful as that of the Evangelical church services. The Peters' displayed faith and hope as Heavenly citizens. As a result, they were able to convince many young converts about living life in preparation for a joyous eternity.

My older brother, Carlo, began attending youth meetings with some of the older teens in the village. Not long after, he became involved in worship services. His interest and influence groomed me into the fellowship. His personality blended among others who were eager to participate in sporting, camping, and other church events. The older members of the Siparia church had envisioned these young men would attend Bible seminary abroad and return as pastors to fill the growing congregation on the island. Winston, Dolan, Harold, Ben, and Carlo were taking some responsibilities in the Sunday school and the youth meetings. However, in the years ahead, some began to walk away from the fellowship and eventually from the Lord.

The remaining few continued to keep active as they grew in grace. Sadly, my brother was not one who chose to remain. His journey of faith with Christ seemed uninteresting for him. Without noticing, he began getting sidetracked by un-churched friends. The company that was influencing him was not interested in a Godly lifestyle. He eventually became the priority on my mother's prayer list, along with the believers at church. During his transition period, the Lord kept me focused in His word growing my faith.

After fifty years of spiritual developing, I still need to grow more in faith. This desire to fellowship is because Christians are *"fellow citizens with God's people and members of God's household, built on the foundation of the Apostles and Prophets with Christ Jesus himself as the chief cornerstone"* (Eph. 2:19-20). My older years have taught me how deceitful are the lust of the eyes, the pride of life, and the pleasures of sin. They are universal temptations to all, including nonbelievers.

They have no respect for age or gender because the objective is to entangle anyone who flirts with sin. I am grateful to God for sending missionaries to foreign lands, especially into societies infested with religious practices like Trinidad and Tobago. Those like the Penners endured an uncomfortable lifestyle at the beginning of their mission work. They adapted to different environments and coped with health issues for the love of God and the people He wanted saved. The Wednesday night Bible study and prayer time was not a practice I willingly adapted to in my new found church fellowship.

However, it was an excuse to get out of the house and meet friends. Then came the dreadful period of sneaking back home. By this time, my Dad had already locked the front door. Nevertheless, my mother would be awake and watching in the galley for me. She kept the side window in the kitchen unlocked. It was through that window I gained access into the house without disturbing my dad. Waking a person under the influence of alcohol can have some serious repercussions. Through the years living at home, the Lord made several arrangements for me to fellowship with His people.

It is helpful for me to remember that once there is a will, there will be a way with God's help. From that tender age of eleven, I responded to His call. The desires of my heart had been weighed, tried, and tested. I now had to consider how best to serve Him and His church. He caught my attention on the crossroads of life one Friday night. The Holy Spirit confronted me about my sins and the need for Salvation. The familiar hymns and choruses they were singing blended with each night's message at the open-air crusade.

Every aspect of the service was centered on the Cross. There were many who responded to the Spirit's calling that night and went forward, each desiring to know more about the depth of love God poured out on us through His Son (Titus 3:5-6). How appreciative I was and still am to know that no one is able to snatch me from Him today. The newly-built lawn tennis court adjacent to Irvin Park Savannah was where the villagers came out religiously every night for fellowship. Each night, one free gift of a painting done during the service would be given out. It went to the person who invited the most amount of people for that night. However, the hour of hearty singing also drew the crowd. Before the Pastor delivered the message, the visiting musical team would perform. One played music on a regular carpenter's handsaw. Another used the Hawaiian guitar to make sounds like a train in motion. As customary, after each sermon, an invitation was given to come forward for counseling. Of course, some went for prayer every night. Others like me wanted to learn more about that free gift of Salvation.

The familiar hymn *"All to Jesus I Surrender"* was sung by the choir. It took courage and determination for me to stand in faith. I placed my trust in the God who offered me Eternal life from that very moment. What was the decision others were making as they went forward? Only the Lord knows. For me, it was about the consequences and pending wrath of God for ignoring, grieving, and rebelling against His Holy Spirit. That night it was settled at the foot of the cross by His grace and mercy.

I am indebted to my friend "Hector" who encouraged and also accompanied me to the alter call. Hector lived two blocks away from my home. He was a genuine friend, although he was much older. His words of encouragement guided me in the path of righteousness. Then, Jesus took me with open arms just as I was into His Royal family (the Church). Sealing me with His blood, I became the *"apple of His eye"* (Zech. 2:8). He guards me like the pupil of the eye is guarded from danger.

Each morning I see my reflection in them when I look into His eyes. Believers sometimes take for granted that Jesus Christ was the first missionary to Earth. Leaving the portals of Heaven where divine holiness was the norm, He condescends in search of a prodigal race. Today His disciples continue to spread the Good News. He is building His universal kingdom (Matt. 28:18-20). With one goal, one vision, and one message to all who are weary, battered, broken, rejected and despised, there is hope. He said, *"I have come that they might have life and that they may have it more abundantly"* (Jn. 10:10).

His Spirit now gives us the ability and assurance to live life more abundantly. The rich young man in the gospel story (Matt. 19:16-22) thought his wealth and decent moral life would grant him access into Heaven. He was not willing to sacrifice his possessions to follow the Lord. Therefore, he went away rich and sad without that assurance. I have grown into a world that is being consumed with things and perishable stuff, most of which have no spiritual benefit to encourage my faith or worship values.

Their magnetizing glow has a craving effect that can produce an occupational habit. With the increase in knowledge also came inventions to pacify the desires of my heart. The Apostle Paul shared his testimony to the saints at Philippi. He said he *"counted them as rubbish the things he gained in this world"* (Phil. 3:7-8). The people of Siparia got the opportunity to hear and make a decision that week. Some with excuses are still seeking contentment and peace of mind today. It is because of this urgency that I'm creating a wave of refreshing memories for all readers.

The uncertainty of going to Heaven, the refusal of God's gift of Salvation, and the issues of life which trouble the unbeliever can be resolved through the peace God offers (Jn. 3:16). His word provides answers for every day challenges and is useful for *"teaching, rebuking, correcting, training, and for every good work"* regardless of circumstances or age (1 Tim. 3:16). I have to constantly remind myself that this journey with Christ is not about speed, nor is it about success in the eyes of others. It is about allowing Him to guide me to the very end of my journey in life.

He said to all who will follow Him, *"I will instruct you and teach you in the way you should go; I will guide you with my eyes."* For this experience to take place on a regular basis, I must be willing to *"forget those things which are behind and reach forward to those things which are ahead"* (Phil. 3:13b with emphasis). As a young man eager to experience life, my unsaved mentors encouraged another belief. Only monetary success can bring true happiness. Maturity in age has allowed me to witness how this deceptive belief has brought many lives unbearable pain.

It has fractured the lives of families, homes, and societies far and wide. I regularly hear of testimonies from those who rejected the gift of God's salvation. This is one of the consequences the Bible mentions: *"He is angry with the wicked every day"* (Ps. 7:11). I was not surprised to hear of this commentary among the world's wealthiest persons. They gathered to discuss global investments and pay respect to the richest among them. After all was said and done, a voice asked, *"What is it that you want now in life?"* Without hesitation, a resounding reply was, *"A little more!"*

Among the lessons I've learned from that response, this one comes to mind: *"Wealth seldom allows its master contentment."* Our modern world of individualism captures the soul that prefers only to exist. In a wave of voices comes distractions and desires for materialism. The lack of pure truth under strenuous worry and depression is always frustrating. However, the Bible says, *"When a man's ways are pleasing to the Lord, he makes even his enemies live at peace with him"* (Prov. 16:7).

I am grateful to have biblical truth as the backbone of all circumstances in my life. It provides the evidence for my victory over both deaths. It heals my troubled heart and calms me when I am depressed. It fortifies a dying life by turning doubts into hope. According to Scripture, our troubled world is not getting better with religions and cultural practices. If it did, we would not be in this predicament today (Jn. 16:33b). There is a subtle difference between a young life and an old life receiving God's gift of salvation.

With a young person, both life and soul are saved. With an old person, only the soul is saved. That life has already lived in vanity and pride. Nevertheless, the grace of God allows them to enter Heaven by the *"skin of their teeth"* (Job 19:26b). It is a popular belief that those who have contributed to the progress of humanity will be justified for Heaven. Over the span of history, millions have done countless hours of voluntary services. Many are responsible for the conveniences and comforts our societies enjoy. In the eyes of man, society accepts them as "good persons."

However, the Bible says it is *"not by works"* anyone will enter Heaven (Eph. 2:9). As a believer of Jesus Christ, I know no one is too sinful for God to forgive. And when He does, this is what He does: *"As far as the East is from the West, so far hath He removed my sins"* (Ps. 103:12). Geography is always an interesting subject for me. I've learned about interesting places, some of which I may never see, but that does not deny their existence. For example, the North Pole, which the American Navy personal Robert E. Peary reached on April 6, 1909, or the South Pole that Norwegian explorer Roald Amundsen reached on December 14, 1911. Our scientists calculated many astronomical predictions with knowledge gained from similar expeditions. The aid of technology gives us daily weather forecasts. However, no one has ever been able to determine the distance between the East and West. History reveals the Ancient Egyptian had no modern technology, yet they were able to calculate the sun was about 93 million miles away from Earth. Today, man is capable of traveling through the cosmos.

He is walking on other planetary worlds in the solar system, but he cannot determine how far the East is from the West to put a flag pole. Man's knowledge has fed his improvised heart with temporary desires, but the Creator feeds his people with the "living Word." His indiscernible, uncontainable, and limitless authority did not prevent His condescension. Nor did His perfect Divinity prevent Him from making footprints along the Della-Rosa leading to Mount Calvary. He eradicated the sting of sin and the grave to set captives like you and me free.

"Therefore if the Son makes you free, you shall be free indeed" (Jn. 8:36). In his epistle to the saints at Ephesus, Paul the Apostle reminds the believers that *"He* [God the Father] *made us* [sinners] *alive together with*

Christ [His beloved Son]. He raised us up together with Christ; He made us sit together in Heavenly places with Christ" (Eph. 2:5-6). When Christ slipped on skin for our convenience, it was for the redemption of a lost race. He shared in the vista of human experiences.

The records of history (Lk. 8:26-30) preserve the evidence that there was such a person. *"Don't allow the demons to know Christ better than you"* (Ps Thabiti Anyabwile). To keep my sanity in tack as a young man without a career, I welcomed doing various maintenance jobs in the neighborhood. Interestingly, there were also designated days at church to do maintenance work. Although the response was not as enthusiastic as the pot-luck dinners, there were faithful believers who came before sunrise to sweat it out.

The work was tedious, but it was fulfilling to fellowship around the breakfast basket provided by the ladies. Other areas of accountability included my tongue and expressions often referred to as body language. These can convey a poor testimony and become a stumbling block to anyone seeking Christ. Often this cliché is used for negative references: *"What goes around sometimes comes around."* I prefer to share what my father taught me, now to my grand children. nieces, and nephews: *"A good name is better than riches."*

In this changing world of twenty-first century pilgrims, societies are bombarded with anti-Christ practices. Knowledge has increased to reach the platform of events the Bible refers to as the times of Armageddon (Rev. 16:16). With the God-given ability to think reason and verbalize our thoughts, there should not be any shortcuts to following instructions in righteousness. Unlike the animal kingdom, I have the ability *"to pray and make supplications"* for others (Ja. 5:16).

God also requires the faithful to *"stand in the gap"* and intercede for others in need (Ezek. 22:30). These are His words to restore my confidence. *"And my God shall supply all my needs according to His riches in glory by Christ Jesus"* (Phil. 4:19). Which other god(s) makes similar promises and renews your hope, my dear unsaved friends? It was in my late teens when I began working as an apprentice at Syne's Contracting Company. The two-mile walk to work was not always as refreshing as anticipated. Nevertheless with hope of accomplishing a permanent job, I did not hesitate to work my probation period for six months without wages.

However, after five months of work and my supervisor's commendation, the company decided to give me a weekly incentive. During the third week on the pay list, I became ill and was not able to walk for a week. This predicament and my mother's concern with the doctor's advice persuaded me not to go back to that type of laborious work. During those weeks, I felt as if the Lord was not going to allow me a permanent job in life. Reading the Bible and memorizing verses like Proverbs 3:5. *"Trust in the Lord with all your heart,"* was a test of faith that I always failed. Nevertheless, I learned to accept whatever the Lord provided as best for me.

Even in times when children fail to realize that they don't choose their parents, this verse will help them through the early years of training. I am blessed to be a recipient of my father and mother's character. God also included their personality and knowledge to perpetuate the cycle of life through me. I **should have shown more** appreciation in *"honoring them"* on a regular basis, not only on special occasions (Col. 3:20). With both our parents deceased after a few years into marriage, my wife and I relied on the Lord for family counseling.

Our new relationship had to be revalued in light of our current circumstances. Any disappointments or physiological pains had to be shelved. We wanted a progressive walk with each other and the Lord. Feelings of self-pity or dysfunctional memories had to cease at the foot of the cross and *"forsake foolishness and live, and go in the way of understanding"* (Prov. 9:6). Whenever I chose not to consider my ways, I usually ended up with problems. The Holy Spirit promises to guide all who will obey Him. When a born again believer chooses to disregard His instructions the consequences can be uncomfortable; it is like having to punish children you love so they will know you are concerned about their wellbeing.

It is true that *"a clean conscience is always a soft pillow."* From the dust to that day when I will return, remind me Lord of your question. *"What is man, that you should exalt him, that You should set your heart on him, that You should visit him every morning and test him every moment?"* (Job 7:17-18). Therefore, Lord, *"teach me to number my days so that I may gain a heart of wisdom"* (Ps. 90:12 amplified). He knew me before I knew Him. In fact, He said, *"Before I formed you in the womb I knew you, before you were born I sanctified you"* (Jer. 1:5).

As many teenagers do, I also took blessings in disguise for granted. Usually they came from simple, friendly folks in the neighborhood. We referred to them as "uncles and aunties," regardless of color, creed, or race. Stern discipline and godly counseling were also integrated as part of my neighborhood. The younger generation accepted them as godly pillars in the community. It was them I went to for letters of recommendation for job applications.

Whenever the rod of correction was enforced on the seat of understanding at any home, the village children rumored the incident at school the following day. However, it did not stop the seasons for embracing and sharing at homes that were opened to all. This is contrary to some societies today where it appears that they have lost those "disciplining bonds" in the new breed of parenting. Un-churched children in modern societies seldom consider themselves to be a reward or *"heritage from the Lord"* (Ps. 127:3).

Perhaps this is why the old African proverb was true and workable in my neighborhood: *"It takes a village to raise a child."* Although Christianity has brought many neighborhoods together, there were some who preferred to remain on the perimeter, searching for counterfeits. As a result, I believe the gospel message is in greater demand for the people of tomorrow. The Lord wisely arranged my early pre-schooling where Bible reading was included as part of the curriculum. I was born into a Muslim and Hindu religious background.

Christian education and biblical principles seemed comfortable for my parents to allow me to accept. They also chose a Presbyterian school instead of other religious schools within walking distance from our home. My family's broad scope of religions can be traced from Saudi Arabia to India. Perhaps this is why so many family members are strongly influenced to hold onto customs and rituals. This heritage has taken permanence over the gospel message and hope of them spending eternity in God's presence.

Nevertheless, here I am years later still attempting to reintroduce this old message of Good News. Because of God's Grace, it is worth the attempt. I will continue trying to build a bridge of communication and earn the privilege of "brotherhood." Through the Holy Spirit's support and guidance, I believe such a bridge will allow Jesus Christ to walk from one heart to another. For it is only by God's grace I can testify of past, present, and future blessings which came not by luck or chance. It is the divine intervention from the hand of providence.

He is Omniscient. He is and forever will be actively involved in all of His creation. Regardless of the evildoers of inequity, He is aware of the spheres of humanity. In spite of all who blame God for the problems the world is currently experiencing, His mercy and grace overrule ignorance. The Prophet Job penned these words, *"Can anyone teach knowledge to God, since He judges even the highest?"* (Job 21:22). I have grown to appreciate these words from Dr. Ravi Zacharias's testimony, which echo a similar heartbeat to mine.

> *I came to Him because I did not know which way to turn and I have remained with Him because there is no other way I wish to turn. I came to Him longing for something I did not have. I remain with Him because I have something I will not trade. I came to Him as a stranger and I remain with Him in the most intimate of friendship. I came to Him unsure about the future. I remain with Him certain about my destiny.*

In comparison to what has come to pass in my life and what is yet to be fulfilled, my offer would be to mold our younger generation to become "fresh thinkers" instead of "selfish seekers." This is a challenge which begins at home and spreads through the church before entering the world. I believe whenever God is totally involved in our lives, the world will hear *"it came to pass."* Do not go the way of the broad road, for too many have regretted doing so (Matt. 7:13). *"For whatever things were written before were written for our learning, that we through patience and comfort of the scriptures might have hope"* (Rom. 15:4).

Chapter Two

WHICH JOURNEY ARE YOU ON?

When I think about making a journey to somewhere I have never been before, my first reaction is to try and find out as much information as possible about that place. It helps to alleviate some of the unnecessary fears that may cross my mind when I arrive. It also allows more time for indulgence with anticipated pleasures. Another thought for consideration would be to prepare the proper clothing and commodities that may be needed based on weather conditions, etc.

I'm sure each person's list of "things to do" will be different and hopefully rewarding. However, because this journey you are about to embark upon is new, it will come with surprises and great expectations. Therefore, it would be wise to put the Boy Scout motto into practice. Similarly, the journey through life from birth to death requires preparation. Each stage of your journey will come with questions, some of which gaze back at you in solitude, such as: Why was I born with these physical or mental challenges? Why do I feel differently than others? If only this or that was different, life would not be so exhausting. Each person's "why" list can be unbearable if there are no guardian adults to echo their thoughts. For me, it was searching scripture when others seemed unreachable. My Redeemer always has time for me. He answers, even if it's a "no" when I want a "yes." To heed His advice is more rewarding than ignoring Him.

Learning to appreciate whatever life throws at me is never a delightful experience. Some days it feels like a roller coaster ride. However, when I consider what the Lord has done for me in the past years, it helps me be content with my present circumstances. One prime example is that of being older with responsibilities and my current status in life. I have grown to the realization that humans of all ages (without the gift of salvation) can become difficult to satisfy at various stages in their lives.

Allow me to explain with a story. An old man and his young son decided to travel by horse to visit family members 20 miles away from their home. His wife died two years before, and he was growing physically weaker in caring for his young son. His limitations caused him to make a decision. It would be in the boy's interest to live with these family members. Early the next morning, they packed supplies for the journey and rode out together toward their destination. It was a four-day's journey that entailed passing through small villages along the main road.

On the evening of the first day, they arrived at the first village with both of them sitting on the horse. The people saw them and felt sorry for the tired, frail horse that carried them 5 miles. With ridicule and frustration, the people accused the old man and his son of animal abuse. Therefore, to please the people, they both left early the next morning. The old man sat alone on the horse for the next five miles, and the boy walked until they arrived at the second village. It was a terrible sight to see the tired young boy struggling into the village at sunset. Once again, the village people complained with bitter remarks.

They felt the old man should walk and allow his son to sit on the horse. After the night's rest, they headed out at dusk with the young boy on the horse. Eight hours later, they arrived at the third village. The grumbling crowd greeted them with suggestions that would encourage them both to walk and allow the poor, frail animal to carry only their baggage. On the morning of the fourth and final day, they left with a guilty conscience. Therefore, they both decided to carry the horse. Arriving at their family's house, the neighbors and relatives came to greet them with scandalous laughter. *"Why carry the horse when you both can ride it?"* the people remarked.

The moral of this story is that you will never be able to please everyone you come across in your lifetime. Another lesson to consider when living among humans (regardless of geographical locations) is that no one is perfect. At every stage of my journey in this life, I will leave behind mistakes. How I learn from them will determine their value. Even Jesus said, *"Unless a grain of wheat fall into the ground and dies, it remains alone; but if it dies, it produces much grain"* (Jn. 12:24).

From the day when I began learning about my Savior Jesus Christ, my understanding about life became more appreciative. Even when the consequences of my earlier mistakes play out, His assurance to be with me to the end gives peace (2 Cor. 1:4). Retaliating is my old nature of handling difficult lessons in life, because they can be unbearable to accept. As a young teen, my view through life's microscope placed me in an unstable position, especially since I had no working skills.

Nevertheless, my heart panted for the experience of independence and self-confidence. How naïve I was in forgetting that "*pride goes before destruction*" (Prov. 16:18). Although I was gaining some working exposure within my community, my foresight for a comfortable journey in life was frightening. During those years, I felt no ray of sunlight to warm my troubled heart. My *double-minded* feeling became my worst enemy (Ja. 1:8). As knowledge increased with age, I thanked the Lord for my parents.

My mother was not Turkish, but she often repeated similar words from that old proverb which says: "*No matter how far you've gone down the wrong road, turn back.*" With the combined experience from both my parents, I know God has provided a wealth of education for me to use. I don't have to put my hand in the fire to learn of the damages it will cause. Fire may be a good servant, but it is certainly a bad master. It is one of the elements chosen by Almighty God to announce some form of seriousness.

Like Love, which will exist for all eternity in Heaven, so will fire reign in Hell for all eternity (Rev. 20:14). Even though we "*all have sinned*" (Rom. 3:23), He has provided an alternative (Jn. 3:16) so no one should be left in a state of paradox. I don't have to fend for myself on judgment day. I chose to change and not remain on that road leading to destruction. He provides contentment, peace of mind, and joy unequivocal to happiness. Some mornings my agenda can be overcrowded with things that may appear to have an urgent appeal. If I am not mindful of the words "*be anxious for nothing*" then in a short time I can feel fatigue.

I am learning to appreciate simplicity, especially when I'm on vacation. The older generation when I was in my teen years knew how to speak to young minds. They lovingly challenged our consciences to participate in the vista of life. Whenever rebellion surfaced, they reminded me of Colossians 3:20: *"Children, obey your parents in all things."* In our village, there were some parents who I thought did not deserve the right of respect. I struggled with accepting what God said, knowing how cruel they were to their children. Nevertheless, God said, "Vengeance is mine" (Deut. 32:35a).

How naïve I was as a teenager to believe that strength and youth will defeat any fear my sinful heart desired. I thank the Holy Spirit for guarding my heart. Some days I felt as if the grass looked greener on the other side of the fence. With His mercy, I understand how maturity can take the rest of my life. I believe God has so many new things in store each day for me to discover, but because of sin, my body is experiencing the process of dying daily. With it comes sickness and suffering. For some, the list can be lengthy.

Salvation from Christ alone comes with abundant life and contentment regardless of circumstances. His reforming is undertaken by replacing the old nature with a new one fit for Heaven. Learning to be observant from the rich, the poor, the young, and the old has helped me to understand when to dot my i's and cross my t's. It has prevented me from repeating mistakes. Journeying the "narrow road" can leave a soul in despair. Often that soul struggles with disappointments and a broken spirit. The Son of God offers daily relief to all in need.

"He made me alive when I was dead in trespasses and sins in which I once walked according to the course of this world, according to the prince of the power of the air, the spirit who now works in the sons of disobedience" (Eph. 2:1-3 with emphasis). Since both *"paths"* in life usually come with trials, temptations, challenges, and rewards, I prefer to go the way that offers a better reward at the end of life's journey. The Spirit of God is committed to helping those who choose the *"narrow path."*

Who will be there to greet those on the *"broad path"* of life's journey? The concept of this truth will eventually face the reality of God's judgment. He said that *"it is appointed for men to die once"* (referring to physical death) but *"after this comes the judgment"* (Heb. 9:27 with emphasis). The security and comforts my academic, social, and financial states have enabled me to enjoy will not acquire or guarantee entrance to God's Paradise. Too many have testified of a counterfeit hope by trusting in perishable things.

This is a common report of those at the entrance of death. In my folly as a boy, I believed it was humanly possible to solve most of my life's problems. With age, time, and knowledge I have been proven wrong. Viewing through the lens of God's grace, I take comfort with these words. He said, *"Not to be afraid of sudden terror, nor of trouble from the wicked when it comes, for the Lord will be your confidence, and will keep your foot from being caught"* (Prov. 3:25-26 with emphasis).

It took a while for me to realize that faith in Christ is not like an insurance policy. His benefits are rewarded now in this limited life and in eternity forever. Contrary to popular belief that the olden days were better for teenagers can be misguiding. It was during my younger years that I witnessed the spread of illicit drugs and the effects of alcoholism. In the growing years I've witnessed how they have become a pandemic concern for all societies and future leaders. Although man has achieved some form of victory with the aid of wisdom, habits are still hard to break.

This is true because our Creator said that *"our hearts are deceitful"* (Jer. 17:9). A pure heart will not lie, steal, or use profanity as their main language. We will not hear the jealously, envy, and reproach of trying to get equal with those we don't like. God's standard for all of humanity is recorded in Scripture. Here are a few words of enlightenment from Psalm 49:16-19: *"Do not be afraid when one becomes rich* which means not to be jealous *when the glory of his house is increased"* (which means do not to envy or crave for such).

This is why *"for when he dies he shall carry nothing away; his glory shall not descend after him. Though while he blesses himself.* (For men will praise you when you do well for yourself). *He shall go to the generation of his fathers, they shall never see light."* I am glad to serve a God whose *"thoughts and ways are not like mine"* (Isa. 55:8 with emphasis). I know how frustrating it can be to wait on the Lord. My plans, ideas, and ways of accomplishing some things are not necessarily how God wants me to proceed.

It is in such moments I find myself debating the sinful desires of my own thoughts to Him. Today, my younger family circle is experiencing similar challenges. All the habits, fashions, and attitudes I've fostered into adulthood now have that reflecting environment of my homeland. It mirrors my desires before Christ to become my new reflection. Someone once said that *"every job is a self-portrait of the person who did it."* Much like many teenagers today, I struggled to defend my own lifestyle. I was not easily persuaded into "considering my ways."

However, after years of following the Lord's disciples who were scattered across evangelical congregations, I saw the need to control my attitude before it controlled me. My mother was one person of instrumental value that the Lord used. She did not spoil this child to spare the fire-stick, broom handle, rolling pin, or anything close in range of use. Those "instruments" of pain kept parts of our bodies well massaged. I felt there were times when our physique was out of alignment. Her favorite proverb was *"How you make your bed, so you will lie."*

Often she reminded me that *"friends will carry you, but they will not bring you back."* She was referring to ungodly friends. The Psalmist writes, *"My son, if sinners entice you, do not consent"* (Ps. 1:10). Journeying from the cradle to my grave will not be defined in one solitary statement. For every stage of maturity there will be different rules that will bring changes. I am learning to depend more on my Savior because He said, *"I will never leave you nor forsake you"* (Heb. 13:5b).

These are the words from the Apostle Paul admonishing the saints in the early church. He said, *"Whatever you do in word or indeed, do all in the name of the Lord Jesus Christ"* (Col. 3:17). I believe for each person's journey in life, scripture is applicable. It was the wise King Solomon who said, *"He who keeps instruction is in the way of life, but he who refuses correction goes astray"* (Prov. 10:17). It is written that *"we must all appear before the judgment seat of Christ that each one may receive the things done in the body according to what he has done whether good or bad"* (2 Cor. 5:10).

God said there will be no shortcuts, no secret bridges, no holy river, or any other manmade method to avoid His final judgment. *"His reward with him to give everyone according to what he has done"* (Rev. 22:12b with emphasis). My first concept about spiritual growth was to try and keep a balanced life. For me it meant maintaining a decent moral character by performing religious objectives. This was not biblical teaching but that of copying from an influx of nine other religious organizations within the community of Siparia.

Each presented a different doctrine with opportunities that could fulfill life's desires. Some taught that *"all roads lead to heaven."* Others proclaimed that *"all religions worship the same one God."* These assumptions caused many to keep jumping pews in search of God. Those who preached justification by works always seemed to have the greater crowd. My search ended when I found out that Jesus Christ is God's Son (Jn. 14:6). The thought of accepting His beloved Son who died for the sins of the world is still rejected for lack of faith.

Worshipers who display a boisterous and mysterious charismatic form of worship contrary to Psalm 95:6-7 display a lack of obedience to Scripture. It is applicable for all to *"worship and bow down; to kneel before the LORD our Maker; He is our God, and we are the people of his pasture and the sheep of His hand."* I never anticipated the time would come to worship in a world crowded with only traditional values. I believe the protocol for worshiping the Holy Risen Savior should always be in conformity to what scripture declares, not what man thinks or feels like doing.

Multicultural worshipers often appear to be maintaining beliefs deriving from the ancient Eastern religions. Christians, however, are instructed to *"worship in the beauty of holiness"* those with *"a pure heart that have not lifted their souls to idols"* (Ps. 24:3-5 with emphasis). The quest for spiritual perfection is not a goal but a process, which Christ is helping me achieve on a daily basis. The ethics of religions often exclude the reason and purpose for Jesus' incarnation. However, His earthly ministry, brutal death, and supernatural physical resurrection have silenced skeptics of all ages.

The fulfillment of prophesies have become vital evidence staining the pages of religious history. His doctrine fosters goodwill and peace and elevates the fear of physical death to all who put their trust in Him. This is what His Apostle Paul wrote from prison in Rome to remind the saints during that era. He wrote, *"Jesus Christ is God's glory with full authority, and every knee will bow, and every tongue will confess that He is Lord"* (Phil. 2:9-11 with emphasis). It is not a mythical belief.

I have heard the discussion among religious practitioners that the judicial scale of God will determine who gets into Heaven. The assumption of good deeds outweighing the bad deeds has turned many hearts deeper into sin. Another religious camouflage is using bible verses out of context for personal gain. Listening to religious street meetings as a young boy, I often questioned their presentation on good works and decent upbringing. It came with 10% biblical truth and 90% manmade fables. I memorized two biblical verses as guidelines in discerning the truth scripture offers.

The first is from Revelation 22:18-19 (with emphasis): *"If anyone adds to these things* [meaning the authentic Devine revelation from God] *and if anyone takes away from the words of this book the* Bible *of the prophecy, God shall take away his part from the Book of Life."* (That book is in Heaven with names from every nation, tongue, and tribe.) The second, from Matthew 28:18-19, is where Jesus commands the apostles before His ascension. He says, *"Go, preach, and teach."*

He specifically said, *"WHATSOEVER I HAVE TAUGHT YOU."* It is why the chosen prophets and apostles wrote what the Spirit of God revealed to them during that 1,500 year window. Only His gospel good news is able to make a difference in my life. In spite of limited financial resources, I was fortunate to attend a few gospel training retreats. With emphasis on bible memorization both at Sunday school and camps, my foundational pillars were secured by God's grace. I take courage amidst the storms of life from Psalm 119:19.

Many have become intrigued and spellbound with the fingertip access of modern technology. When Satan said to Adam and Eve that they will become as gods, He wasn't joking (Gen. 3:5). With the growing of civilizations, the "broad way" of life has attracted busybodies. There is limited room in our hearts to hide scripture. Mortal man often forgets that *"we do not wrestle against flesh and blood, but against principalities, and powers, against the rulers of the darkness of the age, against spiritual hosts of wickedness in heavenly places"* (Eph. 6:12).

Modern congregations have shelved the command for scripture memorization. It is natural for unsaved persons to be blinded from the spiritual warfare that is raging. In recent times with the advancement of technology, distractions have become more enticing. Some of which adds to the busyness of everyday existing. The unsaved get occupied because they *"walk in the counsel of the ungodly, they stand in the path of sinners, they sit in the seat of the scornful"* (Ps. 1:1a with emphasis). This natural stage of declining from walking to standing and then sitting is a result of *"men loving darkness rather than light"* (Jn. 3:19).

My old nature as referred to in the Bible *"encourages me to turn away from the truth and listen to fables"* (2 Tim. 4:4 with emphasis). However, Jesus promises to *"instruct us, teach us, and guide us"* (Ps. 32:8). Upon completion of elementary school, there was no urgency from my parents or older siblings to encourage me with my education. Therefore, I began to indulge in various activities with friends in the neighborhood and at church.

I developed a passion to work with my hands in the areas of arts and crafts. Two brothers in the faith, Andrew and Kelvin, had a similar agenda, since we were unemployed. We enjoyed the days spent beneath the church building engaging in table tennis, boxing, knife throwing, and weightlifting to name a few hobbies. As the years increased with nothing to do and plenty of time to do it, we stretched our minds learning wood and leather crafts. When Mr. Penner came to shepherd the flock at Siparia Church, he introduced archery and camping to the youth group.

His knowledge and experience in carpentry was also shared among us whenever we visited his home. His friendly personality won the hearts of many others who attended church services and youth meetings. On several occasions my mom allowed me to swim with him and my two friends. Our regular places were Mora Dam, Morugia beach, and Quanim beach. A few years before the Penners left, Mr. Penner began to build a log cabin close to seaside in Morugia. He used Teak logs bought from the Forestry Department in Morn Diablo.

We journeyed and worked all day on Mondays for months to see it completed before they headed back to Portland. Andrew and his bride were fortunate to spend their honeymoon there before it was sold. We also enjoyed cycling seven and a half miles to Quanim beach and ten miles to Los Iroes beach on weekends. To the back of the church on the hilltop was a footpath used as a shortcut for members attending church. Most of the surrounding land belonged to the government or was referred to as Crown land. People were allowed to occupy it on a temporary basis for agriculture purposes. No permanent dwelling structure was supposed to be erected on it.

While some grazed their animals, others made kitchen gardens. The young group took advantage when the opportunity presented itself to go hiking, treasure hunting, and using it as a shortcut to Quanim beach. Another activity that was full of excitement for the group was walking the three miles (one way) to Mora Dam. However, for me and my friends during our regular weekdays, we hiked through the private citrus fields before ending up at the water's edge. Then my faith was put to the test. I had to depend on a log from an old tree that fell along the water's edge. It was a typical beginner's method of learning to swim at that dam. The hours spent in the dam developed my ability to swim. After a few weeks, I gained confidence and was able to swim without it. Only then was I able to join the others in making the 400-yard journey to the opposite side of the dam. Although we knew of the alligators occupying the shaded uncut water edges of this reservoir, we did not hesitate to go ashore in search of fruits.

This trip to the dam was adventurous for me and my two nephews, Farouk, and younger brother, Najuib, who were living in close proximity to the dam. However, there were others like Harrylal, Danny, Rohan, Andrew, Kelvin, Percy and more who joined us when they were not occupied. These were the elite group along with several girls who attended youth meetings on Friday evenings at the church. Some of the girls eventually got married to some of the boys who attended the youth meetings and continued attending the church for years. Access to this restricted area was through a private road made for the Caribbean Utilities Company. This manmade dam is still kept in circulation as a reserve today.

During the dry season months, the Electricity Company used the water for cooling the turbine engines at the plant. There were several paths through the bushes, which also led to this reservoir. Many of the village people went there to fish, swim, and collect water for animals grazing near the dam. During some public holidays the youth group would gather for picnics and sporting activities upon the hilltop savannah area. Out initial meeting spot was at the church yard. Some choose to walk while others came packed in Mr. Penner's Victor Vauxhall car.

The quiet, shaded hilltop provided an atmosphere for volleyball, roasting hot dogs, and singing around a campfire. This type of fellowship was always preferred, especially with the newly visiting youths. Some would have remained "liming" on the streets, gambling, or frequenting the liquor bars. Siparia was a community that had a little of both worlds. There were many business and religious establishments that supplied the public's demand. There was one liquor bar, locally called "rum-shop," to every church building within the district of Siparia.

My mother would remind me that *"idle hands are the devil's workshop."* My father made sure that my hands were kept busy; they were even pre-booked for weeks. Nevertheless, this did not prevent me from attending church services. I found time for the things that were most important to me. There were nights when I had to quietly climb through the kitchen window to get into the house after services. My father's bedroom was strategically situated at the entrance of the front door. Therefore, access to the entrance and exit through his bedroom was difficult. Whenever he was under the influence of alcohol, he locked the door before going to bed. His restraints did discourage me at times, but never stopped me from studying the Bible. The Psalmist said, *"His delight was to meditate day and night in the law"* (Ps. 1:2). This is also a good prerequisite for any young believer.

Over the maturing years, the Lord continued to impress upon my heart the type of journey I would be embarking upon. I knew it would be challenging, yet at that young age, I thought it not important to consider. It became my silent prayer request for years, until I allowed the Lord to continue working in my life. Today, after fifty plus years along the same journey, He's still challenging me with surprises. Some of them are from family members scattered here and abroad. During those years of waiting, I learned how to camp out in "His Word." The transition from sinner to saint usually takes a lifetime. I know now that He requires faithfulness before success.

The wisest man that ever lived once said, *"Much study wearies the body"* (Ecc. 12:12b). He did not mean that *"folly is better than wisdom."* Therefore, I should aim towards *"the prize of the high calling in Christ Jesus"* (Jam. 5:11). The writing of Proverbs has become my favorite book. Its practical, everyday teachings have taught me more about submissiveness than any sermon I have ever listened to. When King Solomon said, *"The fear of the Lord is the beginning of knowledge"* (Prov. 1:7), I believe he was referring to my attitude adjustment.

This fear he identifies with brings to mind a submissive heart. It will incur changes that cannot be attained through academic studies. It is applicable to all who are not proud or boastful. The Lord through King Solomon is saying there is only one way to experience His fear. It is by *"taking heed according to His Word"* (Ps. 119:9). In my neighborhood, children were taught to show respect to God and not use His name in vain. Regardless of one's religious practices, it was not acceptable to disrespect other religions.

My *"fear of the Lord"* grew stronger every time I saw or heard of natural disasters. The louder the thunders and brighter the lightning, the more I "feared" the Lord. It takes time to acquire a heart of understanding and patience. To *"keep it with all diligence, for out of it will come the issues of life"* (Prov. 4:23). Contrary to selfish thoughts, a productive journey begins when God's Holy Spirit is leading. Biblical history reveals humanity drifting further apart from the Creator. With every new generation, it appears that the gap has become wider.

Rebellion seems to be one of the main pry-bars that have helped maintain this wedge. During my teen years, it seemed as if most problems were occurring to me. Now, as a past participant with some experience, I can use them as a leverage to share with those who will listen. The wear and tear of competing often comes with emotional and spiritual fatigue. God says, *"Godliness with contentment is great gain."* It can also contribute to longevity. One of several complaints is the cost of living is too high. The Lord provides, and we fail to realize that our living is what is costing too much. When my brain tells me something makes sense, my heart lets me know if it is what I really want. I have come to realize that living with less is not about losing out on options, rather it's about what I have gained. When my heart is overwhelmed and I cannot hear your voice, Lord, allow me to hold onto the truth. I have found that little is much when God is in touch, especially when the influence of evil is pervasive.

I have listened to educated minds that prefer to accept formality as a substitute for actual reality. *"God is often considered by modern thinkers to be just a little better and a bit more stranger than today's man"* (Pastor Josh Manley). My foolish choices have left me with memories of spiritual scars. Christians can also learn a lot from the demons. The first lesson is in obedience to the Lord God (Lk. 4:33-35). Sometimes the truth is hidden in plain sight, just as it is difficult to present the gospel before religious people.

As the blame game of Adam continues, God rich in mercy continues to search for us. I have found out that a wrong attitude can rob me of discretion, understanding, and education in righteousness. God says, *"Every way of a man is right in his own eyes"* (Prov. 21:2a). God spoke through Micah the prophet regarding the controversy the children of Israel were experiencing. He said, *"He hath shewed thee, O man, what is good; and what doth the lord require of thee, but to do justly, and to love mercy, and to walk humbly with thy God"* (Mi. 6:8).

Their "limited edition" of God's law was sufficient to accompany them on their journey to the Promised Land. We have the entity of "sixty-six books" in several languages for every phase of our journey in life, and we cry out for more from God. The Apostle Paul was no stranger to pain and suffering. He had to be content with a thorn in his flesh. The Lord told him, *"My grace is sufficient for you, for my strength is made perfect in weakness"* (2 Cor. 12:7-9). If God's grace was not sufficient for Paul, he would have crumbled under temptations.

He would have stopped his discipleship journey to remove the thorn in his flesh. As often as it takes, I have to humble myself and learn to live with the "thorns" in my flesh. God's truth, not man's opinion, should be the deciding factor along my journey. When I make mistakes, I go to the Lord for strength to recover. The foolish person will continue to practice his folly, because *"it seems right to him"* (Prov. 12:15). Sometimes my old retaliating nature wants to depend on the instinct of humanism for daily guidance.

Believers in Christ have the ability to reason from scripture unlike *"a simple man [who] believes anything"* (Prov. 14:15). Christians depend on *"every word that proceeds out of the mouth of God"* (Matt.

4:4). Growing older has given me a desirable taste for heavenly aspirations every day. I do not have to go back to feelings and experiences, *"for where sin abounds, grace is much more abounding"* (2 Cor. 9:8 with emphasis).

Before the fall, the environment was perfect. That became the order of each day for only God knows how long. We can only imagine. Now join me in a walk through this Garden of Eden. Allow your mind to encapsulate its beauty. Smell the fragrance of early morning aroma as you listen to the chirping of exotic birds. Observe the springs, rivers, and majestic waterfalls with their pure crystal-clear waters. Streets paved with gold and countless precious stones adorn Heaven. An abundance of animals scatter across the land, all living in harmony. Grass flowers and a variety of vegetation plant in blossom with a kaleidoscope of colors in breath taking sight. Males and females of all species are refreshed every morning with an ambiance of gentle breezes. Treetops swirl with joy, as the mountains shout out praises.

It was the abundant life inherited for this couple, which came without stress or worry. They were not in harm's way of any earthly disasters. No fear or lack of want with ageless replenishment. Truly a day in Paradise is certainly worth more than a lifetime on Earth. God's divine intention for all of His creation was nothing short of a miracle of pure joy.

We are told that before the rampage of sin, the Triune God walked with man (Gen. 3:9). Then after his disobedience, man has been busy inventing shortcuts to remedy the curse of pain and death. Man is spending most of his days trying to remove thorns and thistles through long hours of toiling and sweating. He is forever "trying to make two ends meet." My Dear unsaved friend, the worries and cares of a troubled soul will never be over until Jesus Christ becomes Lord and Savior of that soul.

He said, *"Come* (just as you are) *and I will give you rest."* Not to try and fix your life before you go to him (Matt. 11:28). A few centuries forward and what I have inherited as a result of this curse blows my mind out of proportion. Habits I adopted as a young man still encourage my desires of the flesh. Although my background and circumstance may have influenced me, it is not responsible for who I can become with the help of the Holy Spirit. The Bible speaks about *"forgetting those things which are behind and reaching forward* (in faith) *to those things which are ahead"* (Phil. 3:13b).

Some experiences can be difficult to forget and unbearable to forgive. Only in Christ alone can this transformation occur from the broad road to the narrow road. The longest journey for some is from the head to the heart. When I am caught up in the "rat race" of life, I remind myself that even if I win, I'll still be rat! Sometimes I like to compare life's journey to a very long, straight road with speed bumps. They are designed and placed for beneficial reasons. If I choose to ignore them and continue at the same speed, much disaster can lead to fatality.

These speed bumps may come in various forms and fashions in unfamiliar terrain. Similarly, I believe the Lord allows a variety of circumstances to be placed at intervals along my journey in life. I can think of three reasons for using this analogy. The first is to reduce speed. I have had days of hasting, worrying, and being overly anxious. Jesus comes along in Luke's gospel and says, *"Do not worry about your life; it is more than food and clothing; do not fear"* (12:22-32 with emphasis).

With a reduction in speed, the second reason would be to observe others journeying along the same road. Jesus reminded his followers that *"they will come from the east-west-north-south and sit down in the Kingdom of God; indeed there are last who will be first and there are first who will be last"* (Lk. 13:29-30 with emphasis). The Apostle Paul gives a list of "to do" in Ephesians 4:1-6 because *"there is one faith, one baptism, one God and Father of all."* Therefore, we are to *"walk worthy - endeavoring to keep the unity of the spirit."*

Now that He has caught my attention, the third reason would be to appreciate, not complain about the surroundings. My mind is where the battle of disappointments takes place, and my words will be the choice of weapons I have to select. Paul reminded the saints in Philippian 4:6 by saying, *"Be anxious for nothing."* King Solomon said in Proverbs 15:13, *"The heart of him who has understanding seeks knowledge, but the mouth of fools feed on foolishness."*

The parable of the prodigal son gives us food for thought about complacency (Lk. 15:13-17). He began considering all the foolish decisions he made the feet of pigs. When he left home, his thoughts were to get as far as possible from his responsibilities. He wanted nothing to do with commitment and leadership duties. He thought with a bit of luck, he would change the untamed world. Christ made that journey to Golgotha so relentless, hearts can be tamed. Only then will the power of the Resurrection be echoed in the portals of Heaven.

Like all followers of Christ, we say daily, *"Nevertheless not my will, but yours be done"* (Lk. 22:42b). The benefits from bible courses enabled me to share in the responsibilities at the church. Teaching the young teens and planning for youth meetings became a desire of my heart. I gained the confidence from these verses: *"Trust in the lord with all my heart, and lean not unto my own understanding, in all my ways I want to acknowledge him, so that He will direct my path"* (Prov. 3:5-6 with emphases).

During my faith-growing years, the Lord challenged me with the duties of eldership. It became extremely busy, since there was no full-time pastor. After the Penners left, the Executive Body of Evangelical Churches of West Indies found works that came on a temporary basis. During that open window of opportunity, two committed ladies came and assisted with the overseeing of the church. Both Ms. Edith Johnson and Ms. Dona Williamson were originally from the United States but no strangers to church planting.

They focused on cell groups in homes scattered in the surrounding districts of Siparia. In the following years of shepherding the flock in Siparia, they presented three candidates to the executive and local church board for the office of elders. Kelvin Perch, Andrew Bessie, and I seemed ripe and fit for this position. Although the flock was small, there were a few wandering sheep. Some were influenced by the bleating goats and cunning foxes. I believe in every gathering, there are those who the Bible refers to as busybodies (1 Tim. 5:13 & 2 Thess. 3:11).

It is a demanding responsibility that should not be taken for granted as advised by the apostle (1 Tim. 5:17). Some left in search of the perfect church, as we found out through home visitation. In the coming years, the Lord provided wives for the three of us. My zeal was flourishing in worship without noticing some unattended issues that began to develop between my new bride and me. I was placing doctrine before duty. This practice caused an imbalance in my spiritual and physical life. More time was spent doing things at the church that could have been postponed.

Became of this overzealousness in trifle matters, I needed counseling to make a healthy transition. Sometimes it helps to step back to get a closer look at what's blocking your view. By God's grace, after forty-two years of "becoming one flesh," my wife and I continue to depend on Him for our daily sustenance. The disciples tell us how busy the Lord Jesus was during his earthly ministry. They said Jesus was up before sunrise, and long after sunset He was healing and casting out demons (Matt. 8:1-6; Lk. 5:40-42).

His compassion for the lost is renewed every morning (Lam. 3:23). As an elder, Sunday school teacher and youth leader, my agenda was crowded. Jesus constantly reminded the disciples of His purpose in coming to Earth. Although He knew of Peter's denial and Judas's betrayal, He kept focused. The trial that lead to His horrendous death was imminent. He spoke of hope and how to love each other. His version of peace was different to what the Roman Empire offered to their citizens. He is acquainted with our grief (Isa. 53).

Like the disciples, some of His followers today have little faith and lots of questions. Jesus knows that without the assistance of the Holy Spirit, no believer is able to do His Father's will on Earth. It was for this reason He came on the day of Pentecost (Acts 1:4 & 5; 2:1-4). Thomas like most of us always had a question. His was *"Lord, we don't know where you are going, so how can we know the way?"* (Jn. 14:5). It has been a rhetorical question for many religious persons throughout the centuries. Some are plagued with fear and confused thoughts regarding physical death. Before choosing a Devine Deity to worship, find out the related historical facts and fundamental principles.

Next would be to know about the authority over the supernatural and physical realms. Make sure that after physical death, an eternity awaits you in the presence of your god. For me, I had to know the extent of my God's capabilities. There are so many options in the religious world to choose from. I should know without doubt that this Deity I chose to worship is the correct one for me. Each seeker has the free will to choose. We are created beings with the ability to reason. Those who believe they are evolved will have difficulty in accepting the word of God as the only Divine inspiration.

Among the questions that wonder through the mind of a religious person, here is one worth considering. Is my faith assuring me of the confidence I place in this God I hope to spend eternity with? Since gullibility is not a Christian virtue, I usually look to the words of Christ for an answer. John the Baptist did not have the written word as we are privileged today, yet he preached, *"Repentance-for the Kingdom of God is at hand"* (Matt. 3:1-3). When Jesus began his ministry, it was about *"Repentance and the Kingdom of God"* (Matt. 4:17). Interestingly, both preached repentance as the main criteria for the Kingdom of God. What is my faith and your faith preaching to this world lost in self-righteousness?

With His physical ascension in the town of Bethany, (Lk. 24:50-51) and His great commission in Galilee, He said to them, *"Go-preach and teach to all nations about the Kingdom of God"* (Matt. 28:16-20). He is the only one given the full Godhead authority to take us back to Heaven. His disciples never visited or lived in Heaven before. The Old Testament patriarchs were commissioned by God, but none of them ever lived there before (except for Adam and Eve). No other religious leader has ever lived there **before**. Jesus Christ knows which journey each person should be on. He is an all-knowing God with the best of heart for each of us.

Here is a scenario based on John 14:6b. To arrive by aircraft on this exclusive island, there are instructions to follow. There is a designated tarmac, aviation, and ground control in place for safe landing. Flying from any destination upon entering Grand Cayman Island, *"the sky is the limit."* Regardless of how many flight paths the pilot may choose to apply, there is only one specified landing strip. Although science and technology continue to defy the laws of gravity, comfort is available where you find it. However, there is only one designated airstrip.

The use of larger aircrafts often provides better convenience and comfort, but instructions cannot be ignored. Today's autopilot elevates the complexity of the mind and allows for less fatigue on pilots and passengers. However, for efficient landing, pilots cannot disregard safety instructions. To refuse will result in chaos and difficult consequences. Specific instructions are imperative for reaching one's destiny. The Bible teaches that Salvation in Jesus Christ alone is the main instruction for entering **His** Heaven.

In His Redemption plan, there are no substitutes or shortcuts for following His instructions. Those who ignore them will be misguided and spend their lives in catastrophe. Here is scenario worth considering:

> *A school child was called into the teacher's office because of striking another pupil. He was exempt from school for two days as punishment. Upon returning, the same student struck the principal and again was exempt for one month. On the day of his return, the Governor of that state visited the school to speak about violence. After the assembly, the student went up to the Governor and struck him in the face. In all the incidents, the motive was the same and the student was the same. However, because of the person to whom this offence was inflected upon, the punishment became much greater. This is exactly how the God of all creation will deal with those who disobey Him* (Ps. Bentley Robinson).

In John 1:1 God declares that "*In the beginning was the Word, and the Word was with God, and the Word was God.*" The "*Word*" refers to "*Jesus Christ.*"

He went back after His resurrection to be with God the Father. The Devil and His fallen angels know it's true (Mk. 16:19; Lk. 24:26; Jn. 20:17). Jesus told His disciples, "*Let not your heart be troubled, you believe in God, believe also in me.*" This is his answer to Thomas and us today: "*I am the way, the truth and the life, no man comes to the Father, except through me*" (Jn. 14:1-6). I am appreciative of Jesus being the "only" way to God, unlike other religious doctrines, which have options on various deities.

Jesus Christ guarantees God's Salvation. Many religious followers live the way Ron Jenson said in his statement, "*I've found a great deal of zest for God's work, but very little passion for God*" Only through obedience to His Word will my allegiance be measured. One of my time-consuming hobbies after marriage and more so now that my grandchildren are part of my daily schedule, is that of photography.

Maturity brings fond memories of God's generosity to those who recognize Him.

In the art of photography, I once assumed the camera's name brand was of paramount importance to the final outcome of its product. Therefore, in spite of my limited knowledge about photography, I should have been able to get the best results. My PHD camera (Push Here Dummy) did come with lots of features and a book of instructions. I eventually found out there is one fundamental school of thought in photography, and when it is neglected, photos will appear, but not in their state of perfection as desired.

This is similar to religious or superstitious beliefs that can generate a degree of almost anything one sets the mind to accept in life. That "broad road" has a similar effect with the capacity to supply a lifetime of distractions. Anything which includes people, places, and things of interest can keep the sinner from recognizing the need for forgiveness. It can invent temporary comforts and cause feelings to fluctuate under abnormal circumstances. God's unconditional agape love not only teaches good humanitarian deeds, it transcends the worth of a soul that should have been separated for Him.

"Our minds are influenced with consumerism that has the ability to cause a drastic shift in values today" (Ps. Thabiti Anyabwile). My objectives before and after marriage have been rearranged to comply with the responsibilities at the time. However, the goal of serving the Risen Christ will never change by God's grace. Along the journey of life, my circumstances did change to enhance my quality of living. In 1988, my family and I packed only our basic essentials and returned to the Cayman Islands.

My work permit was approved as an auto mechanic with a private garage. The mixed feelings of transition we had to endure lingered longer than the job intended. Nevertheless, the Lord was in charge and had other plans for us. Due to health reasons, we left Grand Cayman six months after arriving. Whenever unexpected concerns surface, I believe my faith is being tested. I find the fiery arrows of doubts piercing my restless heart. My thoughts play havoc with devilish questioning. The past decisions begin flashing across the pages of my mind.

Doubts and despair join arms to discourage my faith in answer to prayers already sealed. Through it all, the still soft voice keeps reminding me to *"trust in the Lord with all thine heart and lean not unto thy own understanding, in all thy ways acknowledge him and He shall direct thy path"* (Prov. 3:5-6). Those months in Cayman made us feel like strangers in paradise. Reflecting on decisions raised questions regarding my faith, like resigning from Texaco Trinidad Incorporate Limited.

We waved goodbye to the fellowship of church and family members. Our creature comforts were little, yet memorable in worth. Letting go to embrace another neighborhood in a distant land can be frightening IF GOD IS NOT IN CONTROL. Nevertheless, the mandate for a new job was an answer to our prayers. Thanks to my niece, Debby, who was residing in Cayman, this new agreement was confirmed. The urgency of this transition was never before experienced by my wife, five-year-old daughter, and me.

Then the Lord stepped in and began to work in mysterious ways. As if to add fuel to fire, we had to leave Cayman unexpectedly. It was six months into the first year's work permit. Unforeseen circumstances and decisions which did not comply with the job requirements forced me to leave. This resulted in terminating the work permit. We were not in a healthy financial position to remain unemployed for the remaining six months. My wife was unemployed, and our daughter was attending private schooling.

Therefore, we decided to return home. My faith felt as if it was in limbo. Due to this predicament, I silently groaned for revenge. My anticipation before leaving home was mounted with high expectations. I trusted the Lord for a smooth transition that would bring fruitful opportunities for my wife and daughter. The Lord, however, was not about to make us the laughingstocks of Siparia, nor was He abandoning us. Another window of opportunity opened while we were visiting my brother Carlo and his family. Debby became instrumental again in securing another job for me. It would be with the Government Civil Service. Carlo and his family were residing on the United States island of Saint Croix. His invitation to come and remain six months, instead of returning home, was an answer to prayer. During which time the next work permit would be available.

Only this job would be with the Cayman Islands Government in the Department of Vehicle and Equipment Services. The months spent with my brother and his family were full of surprises.

Some experiences we hope never to get again in this life. I was fortunate to assist with small jobs in the neighborhood. With generous friends we met there, monetary gifts added toward our passage back to Cayman in November 1989. The Lord, rich in mercy, allowed a category five hurricane to sweep through that island in September before we left. By His grace, our house and family members were spared from devastation. We weathered the outcome of Hurricane Hugo's destruction for two consecutive days. However, the majority of the houses on the island were destroyed due to the intensity of the hurricane. After the devastation came the revealing of wicked hearts that were unleashed. During the next three days and three nights, Saint Croix became the land of the lawless. The darkness began to reveal thieves roaming the streets. The law enforcement agents were outnumbered and kept a low profile. Hurricane Hugo did not completely destroy all the buildings. However, immediately after, gangs began vandalizing properties.

These malicious acts continued until the United States Law enforcement arrived. They implemented a dusk to dawn curfew with serious implications to anyone in breach of the law. Both air and ground military were dispatched on the streets with orders to shoot on sight. The Lord continued supplying our needs, as we cued in line daily for food rations. With the aid of the United States Government personnel, residents were being cared for in a safer environment. The return of amenities for every day conveniences, such as water and electricity, took about two months for some.

The long-awaited day finally came to pass in October 1989. We bid farewell to new friends and families, hoping to arrive in time for my new job. It would be at the Department of Vehicle and Equipment Services or Funding Scheme as previously named. This job provided better health and financial benefits with a foreseeable future work permit. With this type of security, we decided to plant new roots there. The Lord eventually orchestrated a job for my wife and schooling for our daughter.

The fleeting years opened wider opportunities in traveling overseas, purchasing land, and eventually building our new house. He also increased my family tree by providing all the necessities for our daughter to begin her own family circle. After twelve years in the field of auto mechanics, the Lord answered another request. This time it was only a change in work within the civil service. A change in congregation became necessary due to the healthier menu we received at the First Baptist Church of Grand Cayman.

The Lord continued to feed us with "every *word that proceeded out of the mouth of God.*" My journey included a fondness for photography. It began in my early adult years and has remained with me ever since, unlike other hobbies that I no longer had the ability to participate in. Therefore, in 1995, I decided to take a correspondence course through the New York Institute of Photography. That certificate became leverage for my work transfer to the National Archive. My prayer petition for a less tedious job enabled me to grow older with a retirement horizon.

Photography challenges me to view creation from various angles and in all seasons without becoming bored. I'm especially fascinated by God's canvasses of sunsets and sunrises. The Psalmist in 89:11 shadows the thoughts of man when he said, "*The earth is full of the goodness of the Lord. By the word of the Lord the heavens were made, all the host of them by the breath of His mouth, He gathers the waters of the sea together as a heap; He lays up the deep in storehouses*" (Ps. 33. 5b-7). "*The Heavens are Yours, the earth also is Yours, the world and all its fullness, You have founded them*" (Ps. 89:11). Again the Psalmist asks this question; "*When I consider your Heavens, the work of your fingers; "What is man that you are mindful of him?*" (Ps. 8: 3a-4a.). Such thoughts remind me not to complain or grumble whenever weather conditions disrupt my personal agenda. Scripture reminds me in John 16:33 that the peace of God is not gained by religious or moral duties. It is a peace not to be confused for quiet time away from a hostile environment. Nor is it a selective period of submissiveness for mental discipline. And it is certainly not achieved with the barrel of a gun. It is peace that surpasses all man's understanding during trials and tribulations, even under difficult conditions. At times, such as during turmoil and disasters, it can be unspeakable or indescribable. When all around seems to be collapsing, the stillness of a peaceful heart shows confidence in the God you serve. It is arguable to believe that some levels of quiet moments come from the aid of the almighty dollar, but it's not the real thing Christ offers unlimited.

Jesus, speaking to his followers, said, *"These things I have spoken to you, that in me you may have peace. In the world you will have tribulation, but be of good cheer. I have overcome the world"* (Jn. 16:33). If our grandchildren who *"are a heritage from the Lord"* (Ps. 127:3a); they will overcome the world's temptations, then I must *"instruct and teach them in the way they should go."* The virtue of patience is God helping me realize He is never late with His delivery to my prayer requests. It is why my heart has to be established upon faith, and not with opinions.

This type of *"faith is the substance of things hoped for, the evidences of things not seen"* (Heb. 11:1). From the quill of the Hebrew writer comes this warning: *"Beware, brethren, lest there be in any of you an evil heart of unbelief in departing from the living God"* (Heb. 3:12). For me, it was when I felt like sitting on a fence wall with one foot in church and the other in the world. Thank the Lord for reminding me that *"No man can serve two masters"* (Matt. 6:24a).

Before His peace returned, I had to remove the apparel of culture and customs after repenting. From then on He reminded me that *"I did not receive the spirit of bondage again to fear, but I received the spirit of adoption"* (Rom. 8:15 with emphases). Many on my prayer list have abandoned the "walk of the cross" for various reasons. Those who are blessed with wealth often fail to realize the need for discipline. Wealth, like fire, is a good servant but can become a bad master. Jesus said it could become a hindrance if you worship it.

Senior citizens of the faith, even those who are less fortunate in wealth, can testify they *"have been young, and now am old, yet (they) have not seen the righteous forsake, nor their descendants begging bread"* (Ps. 37:25 with emphasis). God constantly reminds all Christians to allow His Son Jesus to address our worries and fears. He said, *"Let not your heart be troubled"* (Jn. 14:1). He did not say don't be concerned. It appears that *"worrying is like a rocking chair, it gives you something to do, but will never get you anywhere"* (Pastor David Beckmann).

The journey of the Israelites in the desert had a price tag of forty years, because they *"walk according to the flesh"* with open mouths instead of open minds (Rom. 8:1). Every step of my journey challenges me to *"work out my own salvation with fear and trembling"* (Phil. 2:12b). The world tells me to think with my mind, but go with my heart. The Apostle Paul encourages believers to walk with humility. He said, *"Let this mind be in you which was also in Christ Jesus"* (Phil. 2:5). Jesus said in Matthews's gospel, *"Learn from Me"* (Matt. 11:29).

On the broad road of life, there are many who have been convinced by misguided opinions. As a result, *"the heart became desperately wicked"* (Jer. 17:9 with emphasis). The warning to the church at Colossi was that *"these things have an appearance of wisdom in self-imposed religion, false humility and neglect of the body"* (Col. 2:23). Jesus said, *"All that is in the world, the lust of the flesh, the lust of the eyes, and the pride of life, is not of the father but of the world"* (Jn. 8:44). As the blind beggar said to his guide, none are as blind as those who refuse to see. This is the hope provided to *"whoso hearkened unto me* (Jesus Christ). *They shall dwell safely and shall be quiet from fear of evil"* (Isa. 55:8 with emphasis). God said, *"the soul that sins will die."* Since then, all generations *"... have sinned"* (Rom. 3:23). The gospel message is for sinners who desire to journey back to the Savior. Ancient civilization has accommodated us with archival literature of both historical and spiritual documents. With each copy came opinions, doctrines, culture, and beliefs propagating a river of values for humanity.

There are individuals who have charted lucrative journeys to establish personal monuments of fame and fortune. Some have chosen a different journey to oppose the values and principles of scripture. Others have encountered phenomenal experiences and pride themselves in unrighteous living. Yet all have sinned and come short of God's glory. The hands that fed the thousands and the feet that walked on water were pierced with nails on a cross for me and you, dear friend.

Jesus spoke with two sisters at their brother's gravesite. He said, *"I am the Resurrection and the life"* (Jn. 11:25). World-renowned religious leaders and brilliant scholars have contributed tremendously to the advancement of humanitarian welfare. Some have paved paths to greater science and technological discoveries. Yet the human race ponders at the entrance of death. Maximus Decimus Meridius, the youngest general appointed in Roman history in AD 176 and Legate of the Emperor's Legion, said, *"What we do in this life, echoes in eternity."*

The question that should tickle our consciences is: Which one of the eternities will hear your echoes? To raise the sensitivity of the hearers in the Corinth church, Paul said, *"I do not write these things to shame you; for the wisdom of this world is foolishness with God, He catches the wise in their own craftiness"* (1 Cor. 4:14 & 1 Cor. 3:19). The Psalmist asked, *"What is man that you {***Almighty God***} are mindful of him?"* (Ps. 8:4a). Peter the Apostle echoes the prophet Isaiah's words in Isa. 40:6b *"All flesh is as grass."* Peter reiterates the same thoughts 1 Pet. 1:24 *"and all the glory of man as the flower of the grass."*

Ever since man left the Garden of Eden, his quest for pure happiness continues. His adventures often take him through the melting pot of occults. There are some who prefer to secretly visit the dark corners of continents searching for insidious rituals to indulge their fantasies. I am grateful for the basic knowledge gained through seeing, touching, feeling, and believing in a hope that stills and fills my sinful heart. It's God's amazing grace on His condition and by His terms that brings me joy.

I can now rest comfortably because *"in Him* (Christ Jesus) *we* (all sinners) *have redemption through his blood"* (Eph. 1:7). The cunning idea of trying to become a perfectionist before approaching the sovereign God, did not work for me or the millions of believers the world over. From the dust of deception, the adversity has been trying to cover this truth. *"… If the son makes you free, you shall be free indeed."* Jesus says, *"No man cometh unto the father but by him."* Therefore, all other methods mankind has introduced over the centuries avail to nothing.

He is the way, (not a way) *the truth,* (not assumptions) and *the life,* (after death) *no man,* (regardless of how great man may think of himself) *cometh unto the Father, but by me"* (Jn. 14:6; & Jn. 8:36 with emphasis). The Apostle Paul wrote, *"Casting down imaginations, and every high thing that exalted itself against the knowledge of God, and bringing into captivity every thought to the obedience of Christ"* (2 Cor. 10:5). God has been gracious and persistent towards rebels like me, as He is to all who go to Him.

One day I will rise from Earth's muddy trails to the golden paved streets because I gave careful thought to my ways. The former C.E.O. for the Coca Cola Company, Bryan Dyson, said in his farewell speech, *"Value has a value, only if its value is valued."* The worth of my soul has been measured, weighed, and valued through the death, burial, and resurrection of Jesus Christ. My spiritual growth continues to develop as I *"meditate within my heart on my bed, and be still"* (Ps. 4:4b with emphasis).

The word of God often reveals the poverty of my spiritual character. Religious practices can sometimes encourage a believer to ignore the gospel's truth. God says, *"If we say that we have no sin, we deceive ourselves, and the truth is not in us"* (1 Jn. 1:8). Wisdom calls me to make choices among the voices that offer the capacity to harm myself and others. *"Sin has the ability to warp my personality out of God's alignment; therefore learning to depend on Him helps me to enjoy the best kind of relationship between Creator and creature"* (Ps. Thabiti Anyabwile).

My life was full of amusements that appeared to be harmless. Some were not necessarily useful or profitable as a new convert. The decision to let go of "stuff" I did not need was a lesson on trust. I am still in that transition after many years of walking with the Lord. The Apostle Paul presents three propensities to challenge my testimony. The first is: *"How then shall they call on him in whom they have not believed?"* The second is: *"How shall they believe in him of whom they have not heard?"* The third is: *"How shall they hear without a preacher?"* (Rom. 10:14). My answer to these questions would be: *"not to forsake the assembling of the saints"* (Heb. 10:25). Making sinners into saints can take decades, so we must *"consider one another in order to stir up love and good works"* in the body of believers. Life can become complacent with frivolous occupational habits if no priority is in place for prayer, bible study, and fellowship. As my journey gets closer to those final steps, visibility is vital.

I am encouraged to keep *"looking unto Jesus, the author and finisher of our* (my) *faith"* (Heb. 12:2a). I know what it is to experience a lukewarm heart that identifies with depression, frustration, loneliness, and rebellion. It encourages you to hold on to clichés and use them as boundaries for your daily ordeals. The guarantee to satisfy any sinner's heart in any condition comes only from the Word of God. It helps me recognize biblical doctrine against fiction. It enables the seeker to turn from fables that facilitate the anxiety of moods.

In those moments, the natural person will believe *"the message of the cross is foolishness to those who are perishing at presence."* The reason this trend of thought occurs is *"because the natural man does not receive the things of the spirit of God, for they are foolishness to him; nor can he know them, because they are spiritually discerned"* (1 Cor. 2:14; & 1 Cor. 1:18). This prayer from King Solomon helps me to appreciative the importance of truth. He said, *"Two things I request of Him,* (that is Yahweh) *remove falsehood and lies far from him."*

Daily, the Lord teaches me how to be content as *"He gives me* neither *poverty nor riches, but feed me with the food allotted to me"* (Prov. 30:7-8 with emphasis). The journey of the enslaved begs this question, *"How long, O you sons of men, will you turn my glory to shame?"* This type of life occurs when I become useless and disgusted with what Christ offers on a daily basis. The children of Israel journeying in the desert thought bread and manna was not enough nourishment; they wanted more (Ex. 16:1-36).

Chapter Three

GROWING UP IS OPTIONAL

As a young, energetic man, the thought of becoming old with gray hair and weak limbs was never a major concern for me to consider. I had the concept that age was mind over matter. That is, if I don't mind, it doesn't matter. Add fifty years to that concept, and the reality of growing older is inevitable. At sixty, I'm realizing that it is still optional to become old. I am experiencing that life offers much to those who are actively growing older.

The aging process has a history that appears older than the beginning of time. This condition was decreed by the Creator and has become mandatory (Gen. 3:17-19). It comes with the sting of death and leaves with a bitter trail of mourning. Regardless of all the age-defying procedures, medical science, supernatural indulgence, and financial status, life is fragile and has limitations. It is my belief that survival should be accepted as the Creator's pleasure to invest in us for His glory.

However, traditions and cultures continue to devalue lives by erecting walls of hostility. Only in Christ am I learning to forgive regardless of differences. It's one of several ways this world will know He's alive. It is why the *"sun should not go down upon my wrath"* (Eph. 4:26). For the Christian, death is no longer a mystery to fear. Teaching about the Kingdom of Heaven, Jesus said, *"I go to prepare a place for you...I will come again for you"* (Jn. 14:1-4).

Forty days after His resurrection, many followers ate, talked, touched, and listened to Him (Lk. 24:21; Mk. 16:19). Someone said that *"God does not believe in atheism, therefore atheists do not exist."* The Bible says that *"even the demons believe and tremble"* because there is only one living God (Jam. 2:19). I am now at the age where bending the knees is not as spontaneous as during my volleyball years. However, one day, every knee will bow in acknowledgement of Jesus Christ as the Son of God (Rom. 14:11).

The oil of humility will give flexibility to stubborn knees and cold hearts in recognition to His Authority (Matt. 28:18). When I was a child, I spoke and understood as a child. When I became a man, however, my thought-processing analyses gradually expanded. I enjoyed my childhood years as I grew up among nieces, nephews, and school friends in the neighborhood. It was a process that eventually challenged me with wishes of emulating my older brothers.

Among the record of events after the fall of man was that ability to grow intimately (Gen. 4:1). This attribute fostered the desires of the heart. Centuries later, the desire to conquer and rule for supremacy continues to trick into hearts for legislation to devalue lives. Man's knowledge and education without the wisdom of God continues to cause problems (Gen. 3:16-19). Parents, teachers, and chaperones have the difficult task of separating those who constantly engage in striving. Ezekiel the prophet was perhaps experiencing a similar reaction with the children of Israel.

He told them, *"The Fathers have eaten sour grapes, and the children's teeth are set on edge"* (Ezek. 18:2). I am thankful there is an antidote to this curse, even though the *"Children of God today are doing according to the customs of the gentiles which are all around us"* (Ezek. 11:12b). His grace is sufficient for all circumstances. From the letters of the Apostle Paul come these words to us, *"Those who live according to the flesh set their minds on the things of the flesh--and cannot please God"* (Rom. 8:5-8).

No one has to remind me how my desires of the flesh can crave for ungodly moments. The fleeting years have had their toll on me striving for unjustifiable reasons. Like an orphan on the road to destruction, I had to constantly pray for changes through God's grace. Because I was *"dead in trespasses and sins,"* I *"walked according to the course of this world"* (Eph. 2:11). Although they bring painful memories from wrong choices, I am not discouraged. I am learning to welcome new challenges from my Lord.

I will always be grateful as a convert to *"grow in wisdom and in statue and in favor with God and man"* (Lk. 2:52). Another avenue that was conducive for maturation came with sporting activities. The cricket and volleyball matches among churches bonded the congregations with jubilant expressions. My days of swimming and cycling were not filled with motionless meditations. God said, "*Let this mind be in you which was in Christ Jesus*" (Phil. 2:5). He allowed His Son, however, to experience the mental, emotional, and physical process of aging.

That is why I want to continue keeping active towards those final days before meeting my Savior. The effectiveness of sports has helped gather peoples of various nations under one umbrella. It has combated conflicts among cultures and nations. It has opened doors and bridges that were once closed. It has brought confidence, comradeship, and self-will to individuals. Those who accept growth challenges will always appreciate life. The Apostle Paul uses analogies pertaining to sports in his writings.

In one example, he said believers everywhere should "*strive for the prize of the high calling in Christ Jesus.*" This can only happen when we "*run with patience the race that is set before us.*" We are to do it by "*forgetting what is behind*" (that would be our old way of living). He instructs believers to "*set your mind on things above*" so we may "*reach forward*" (Phil. 3:9-14; Col. 3:2). Similar to physical sporting events, my spiritual race welcomes supporters. The Lord instructs all believers to pray for one another without ceasing.

I know that the prayers of righteous believers have helped me when I was tempted to trust my own heart. My heart has that tendency to rely on presumptuous feelings because my "*heart is desperately wicked*" (Jer. 17:9). When I choose to close my mind to the (gospel) truth, I often land on an open frontier. This is why "*I was glad when*" my friends Kelvin, Andrew, Harrylal, Danny, and many more said to me, "*let us go into the house of the Lord*" (Ps. 122:1). Not only was this on Sunday mornings, but also during mid-week for bible study and prayer.

Reading the Bible regularly can scare the Hell out of anyone. It gives admonition to parents and caretakers about "*training up*" children. I thank the Lord, my parents, and older siblings that did not allow me the option of going down the wrong path in life. You don't have to be a born-again Christian to know the consequences it will reap. Using television and other forms of media devices to supervise children can be an unhealthy substitute. While discipline is an educational task of wisdom, caretakers have the opportunity to reason with the offenders about their consequences.

My mother frequently reminded me of this proverb, "*Knowledge is pleasant to the soul; it will deliver you from the way of evil, it gives discretion and understanding to keep and preserve you when it enters your soul*" (Prov. 10:12 with emphasis). Yesterday I was a child; today I'm a man learning to grow my own family. Never before did I consider how time consuming this responsibility would be because "*foolishness is bound up in the heart of a child*" (Prov. 22:15a). I have come of age to realize that you do not have to teach a child to do wrong things.

King Solomon said that "*God has made man upright, but they have sought out many schemes*" (Ecc. 7:29). Reminiscing over my childhood days brings a taste of mixed memories. Nevertheless, through them the Lord "*worked all things for good for me; because I love Him and is called according to His purpose.*" (Rom. 8:28 emphasis added.). King Solomon continues to remind us that "*wisdom preserves the life of its possessor*" (Ecc. 7:12).

The Lord makes me sensible of my weakness, so that He can pour His strength upon me. This is why "*whatever my hands find to do, I try to do it with all my might, because I realize that there is no work or device or knowledge or wisdom in the grave where I am going*" (Ecc. 9:10). My satisfaction in life will come when I am "*walking in the light*" (Eph. 5:8) "*abiding in Him*" (Jn. 15:4) and learning to "*follow Him*" (Matt. 9:9). I was taught by my mother to respect the worship period and "*behave wisely in a perfect way*" at church (Ps. 101:2).

Today I'm encouraging my grandchildren to "*enter into His gates with thanksgiving and into His courts with praise*" at the place of worship (Ps. 100:4). These next lines are from an unknown author who gives us a paraphrase of the well-known Psalm 23. "*The TV is my shepherd, I shall want more. It makes me lie down on the sofa. It leads me away from the faith, it destroys my soul. It leads me in the path of sex and violence for the sponsor's sake. Yea, though I walk in the shadow of Christian responsibilities, there will be no interruption, for the TV is with me. Its cables and remote control, they comfort me. It prepares a commercial for me in the presence of my worldliness. It anoints my head with humanism and consumerism, my coveting runneth over. Surely, laziness and ignorance shall follow me all the days of my life, and I shall dwell in the house watching TV forever.*"

How true this concept is practiced in some homes where viewers have become addicted. I have to guard from becoming a victim of this modern century plague.

In another context of concern about children comes this paraphrase from an unknown author. *"Last night, my little boy confessed to me, some childish wrong; and kneeling at my knee he prayed with tears: Dear God, make me a man like my daddy -wise and strong; I know you can. Then (the father says) while he slept; I knelt beside his bed, confessed my sins, and prayed with low -bowed head; Oh God, make me a child like my child here, pure and guileless, trusting thee with faith sincere."*

This is an appeal in which I need to *"find grace to help in time of need"* (Heb. 4:16). The moral law is able to curfew my heart temporarily, but *"grace and truth which came through Jesus Christ"* will supply the permanent solution (Jn. 1:17 with emphasis). So then, I should not place value on the years I've lived, but rather value the life with the years He's blessed me with. Our world government leaders are scrambling for remedies with *"empty words which are deceiving the younger generations"* in every broken society (Eph. 5:6 with emphasis).

They are propagating fresh promises of hope, while canvassing for a utopian paradise gained with blood and tears. The Lord Jesus cautions his children *"not to be partakes with them"* (Eph. 5:7). To grow in the Christian faith requires you *"no longer walk as the rest of the gentiles walk, in the futility of their mind"* (Eph. 4:17b). There is much to consider from these words by Steve Jobs. It was his 2005 Valedictorian speech at Stanford University. He said *"Your time is limited, so don't waste it living someone else's life."*

Sadly, I did not realize the implications of that statement until I stepped into the rings of matrimony. I am one among six-billion people who is uniquely designed (Gen. 2:7). I was definitely not here before in time, nor are there plans for me to return after death. The present status is no replica for my identical personality, character, physical abilities and thoughts. Although I have brothers, no one was created with identical characteristics. That means my journey in life is not a gamble.

I don't have to depend on chances or take risks. The Creator has predestined a course that will take me back to Him. With Salvation and faith, the same offer is available to all who want His grace. When we begin training a child to find the Savior, it requires self-discipline, compassion and most of all patience. *Do as I say but not as I do* is not one of the prerequisites for such a job. I find it confusing when adults send their children to Sunday school or church, but they don't see the need to attend.

They recognized the valuable teaching and its benefits for a productive life, yet they can't take the time or show the interest to attend. The silent statement adults are saying is *"I love my children and want them to learn about God and go to Heaven, but I prefer to go to Hell."* The reality of death has not yet synchronized with the time they have remaining alive. Although Jesus knew Peter and Judas were going to betray Him, He did not change the time or the circumstances regarding His journey to the Cross. Instead, He allowed their plans to continue.

Both end results brought Glory to God the Father (Matt. 26:34). The gospel message which included His teaching, preaching and healing ministry is about "the Kingdom of God" and doing His Father's Will. He is not a God of chance, luck or coincidence. His intervention does not depend on human intuition. We mortals don't possess those attributes of Omnipresence and Omniscience. With the help of the Holy Spirit, I can now learn to love others. Before, love was conditional and limited, depending on circumstances.

Before the demons came out of the man, according to Matthew's gospel, they begged Jesus not to send them back to the abyss (Matt. 8:28-34). The devil uses similar tactics to disrupt the order of worship. Pastor C. J. Mahaney suggested that when such becomes the norm of our worship, we are *"basing our relationship with God on our own performance."* Those who perform commercial worshiping to itching ears can become a stumbling block. This happens when quality time is not spent in the Word.

My journey into manhood appeared to be different in comparison to some of my male family members. My Christian faith stood out like a sore thumb whenever the relatives gathered for special occasions. I had yet to learn what King Solomon meant when he said, *"There is a time for everything and a season for every activity under the Heaven"* (Ecc. 3:1-NIV). My short version for maturity is *"not to give a razor as a gift to a seven year old boy."* Nothing is wrong with giving a razor; it's just the timing is wrong. Wait until he is of age to appreciate and be accountable for using it.

King Solomon had a divine privilege of experiencing life in many areas. God granted him a heart of wisdom, so he was able to view life through the lens of wisdom. His conclusion was that without the hand of God's intervention, life eventually becomes meaningless (Ecc. 12:8). It is why he said all is vanity. With spiritual and physical growth comes a variety of disciplinary measures. While it is never comfortable, its achievement should prevail. I have introduced my grandchildren to two ways of getting things done.

Those choices are: the easy way or the hard way. Learning should always be an ongoing adventure for all who delight in living. This bit of experience came to me when I visited the Magistrate Court in Siparia for the first time. It was the place to see how education is not as expensive as ignorance. I learned how the Judge had authority of the full arm of the Law. Therefore, when his appeal for order came across the room, every race, creed, gender, just, unjust, religious, agnostic or atheist that was present complied respectfully.

There was no sudden outburst, grumbling, whispering, phone use or any form of distraction allowed during the proceedings. It was such a day that begged this question: If utmost respect is given to mortal man who is in a temporary position of authority, why not the same from those (believers) who enter a place of worship? (Ps. 100:2). Whether it is attending funerals, weddings or any type of religious proceedings, the general public (usually) complies with respect. My ongoing prayer is for family and friends to pay homage to Jesus Christ as their Lord and savior.

The plague of cell phones, toys, electronic gadgets, crunching and munching comes with distraction. They have become the peril of modern-day worshippers in some gatherings. While it may be the norm for blind seekers who are trivial worshipers to allow such disrespect, *"joint hears with Christ"* should know and do better by example. To be little-wisdom is mere ignorance in the presence of another (Rom. 8:17). Growing older has become a pondering thought, one that begs the question as to where the Lord is going in my life.

Not every day of my life is marked by His aggressive love for others. When things don't seem to go according to my convenience, I have to slow down and seek guidance. I recall seasons as a young leader when my life was becoming spiritually bankrupt. It started when I began adopting shortcuts in presenting the Word of God. Neglecting to study the word can cause spiritual blindness and leave you *"standing at the crossroads"* in search of the ancient paths (Jer. 6:16). This neglect sneaks up on a believer like a thief in the night.

While *"the preparations of the heart belong to man, the answer of the tongue is from the Lord"* (Prov. 16:1). I was warned with proverbs 1:22a. *How long, you simple ones, will you love simplicity?"* I am learning the difference between knowledge about Him and the knowledge of Him. My younger years of strength and vitality boasted themselves through the "no pain-no gain" manifesto. I have gained the investments at the gym on a regular basis. Like all other sports, it demanded discipline and commitment.

Never did I conceive that *"the world and its desires will pass away, but the man who does the will of God lives forever"* (1 Jn. 2:17 NIV). Since I had no intention or desire of dying soon, the alternative was to find out about His will for me, although at that young age I thought the will of God was carried out by only pastors and missionaries. This was not for me, since I had no form of independence living with my parents. Nevertheless, I realized the first step towards knowing God's will was to obey my parents.

This step of obedience comes before any type of spiritual engagements at church or going to mission field. The apostle Paul had this to say about children in the church at Ephesus: *"Children obey your parents in the Lord"* (Eph. 6:1-3). There are no buts or ifs, just simply obey. This topic was hammered upon by un-churched youths who attended summer camps. My silent thoughts were *"it was better for me to obey than feel the rod of correction."* The apostle Paul reminded fathers of the heritage they received from the Lord (Eph. 6:4).

Even though my Dad had another agenda in life, my mother was influential through her devotion to the Lord. Without this, my life could have become futile when I entered the work place. In 1972, I was employed with Texaco Trinidad Limited in the Southern division at Forest Reserve Fyzabad. It was the second time I came face to face with harsh and boisterous working men. I thought they wanted no part of God or His followers. With a troubled spirit, I remembered Bible verses like Romans 3:10-12. *"There is none righteous, no not one; there is none who does good, no not one."*

I began to understand what the Lord was saying as I mingled among my coworkers. His words became more transparent in the lunch room. I was concerned about my testimony as a Christian coming under attack. Some days I felt like a square peg in a round hole. It took some months before I began to realize this would be my "mission field" in serving my Lord. Stepping out of my comfort zone was not as easy as I anticipated. Nevertheless, the Lord did answer my prayer with a permanent job.

I had no room for grumbling like Jonah who become judgmental. I should not (inwardly) condemn them but live up to what I preached and taught at church. *"Christ in me the hope of Glory"* (Col. 1:27b). The prophet Jeremiah advised his secretary Baruch in chapter 45 *"not to succumb to the temptations of ambition, but to be content with his lot"* (Vsr. 1-5). To be content among ungodly co-workers was a lesson in the making that God prepared for me. To become comfortable and accept their lifestyle was not a choice from the Lord.

I realized the subjective truth from the word of God was not what they wanted to hear. Nevertheless, I was not about to compromise my biblical principles to accommodate their pleasurable habits. I thank the Lord for having a remnant of His people scattered in every dark corner. In the following months of employment, I met other believers who were assigned to various sections in the department. The few and faithful worked in harmony among the others who were added to my prayer list.

Those believers gave encouragement to strengthen me during the seventeen years I worked at Forest Reserve. The transport department's lunch room also served as a changing room, but it was not restricted to gambling. Therefore, it was common to hear derogative words anytime a group gathered to wait for another work assignment. Whenever I was in company, there was some who refrained from swearing. I am always thankful to the Lord for such privileges. It is another reason for me to know my doctrine and be ready to share it with confidence.

It was an employment that varied in progression from general laborer to chauffeuring in that department. After twelve years, another transfer to the mechanical department lasted five years before I tendered my resignation in 1989. With the full completion of my Auto and Diesel mechanic craft course, I was able to make another attempt for transfer again. This time it was with a view of migration to the Cayman Islands. However, one co-worker who vowed never to give up his religion of Hinduism got converted to Christianity.

It was a short while after I left the oil company when he informed me of his conversion. Our daily conversations and answer to my prayer eventually came to pass. I recall the hours we spent beneath vehicles in dialogue that continued weekly over the years we worked together. He eventually recognized, by God's grace, the truth that scripture offers against the writing from the Gita. He is serving the Lord at his home church in Fyzabad. The Lord eventually saved his wife and is speaking into the hearts of his children through their example.

Circumstances are always shifting, but God's word never changes. I have learned it is easier to declare my faith to co-workers as early as possible. Waiting to settle in and hoping for the right time can become intimidating. If there is time for mocking, let it be early. Let the novelty of their folly wear off, and eventually they will accept me for who I declare to be. The journey of a Christian may appear to be difficult; sometimes it may assume to become discouraging, and every so often, it brings questions to test your faith.

When such is the case **then considered to be normal** for those who are growing in their faith. However, contrary to the temptations that enslaves and captures a person; only the saving grace of the Son of God is able to free that soul. In past years of experiencing life, I have by nature adapted into habits that can be difficult to let go. Some of which may appear to be good but not necessary the best to maintain as age spotlights its values. Whatever prevents me from serving the Living God on a daily basis, I have to consider it or them as idols. This may not be the same with others who have a different agenda journeying life's path. However, to each choice we make the circumstances will vary, but there will always be consequences to our choices.

This is why our Creator made provision before we were born. He knew how weak and defenseless we would be against the *"wiles of the devil"* (Matt. 26:41). The cunning craftiness of the devil is to prevent as many from learning about God's provision; the same message Jesus came preaching about (Eph. 4:14). I know of the tendencies to become reluctant and disregard my options in growing stronger in my faith. But for the grace, my life could have turned into a fairy tale similar to that of Peter Pan. That is a delightful children's story about a boy whose wishful thinking was to never grow older. He preferred to remain in a make believe world that became his very own "never-never land." It was the ideal place to have his fantasy dreams come to pass and becoming the center of attraction.

He had no realistic responsibilities or obligations to anyone. This trend of wishful thinking became Peter's boundaries where illusions never ended. However, if Heaven is your ultimate objective, then this life style should not be your pursuit in life as a follower of Christ. The title P. P. S. ("Peter Pan Syndrome") is appropriate for those who have no desire to be a leaders or role model in life. While the world has great leaders and role models, some fathers and mothers are still on the bar-wagon with Peter-Pan as their mentor. It is a journey likened to a merry-go-round cycle, with no desire to stand firm on the Solid Rock. At Peter's age, mental growth becomes optional for him to do as he pleases. In affluent societies that are changing rapidly, Peter will struggle for supremacy to dominate those under his domain.

He wants no part of sound discipline. His initial intension is to have no commitments or challenges in becoming realistically responsible. They would only jeopardize the childish routine of Peter. However, mature adults are expected to contribute to the welfare of humanity. Regardless of culture or beliefs, no man is an island. People need people in times of emotional and physiological pains. From the day we're born we begin to die, so life is in transit. Christians are expected to *"take up our cross and daily follow our Lord"* (Matt. 10:38 with emphasis) while the unbelieving crowd consider following Peter's world of oblivion.

My childhood years of pain and sorrow, joy and laughter are basic elements that will continue throughout my life. They contribute towards maturity in the cycle of a person's life. While our youth is for learning, our understanding comes with aging. To encourage mental and spiritual growth, I have to let go of fantasy and hold on to reality. Life in Christ begins when a person reaches the end of their comfort zone. I had to stop inhaling the dust of procrastination and take a leap of faith. One of those steps began when I decided to travel abroad with my family.

It was commonly advised by older folks in my village; before marrying take the opportunity when it comes to travel the world. Not that one air-fare is cheaper or a room with a view would be less expensive as a single person; but they knew the responsibilities that come with marriage. As a young married man, I never anticipated traveling or residing abroad due to my education. Applying for a United States visa from my country with my limited resources was not sufficient requirements to obtain a visa. With a decent job, a new bride, our first home, a vehicle and the love of our life, a baby girl; we had little hope of moving to another beautiful, tropical island.

Yet God rich in mercy provided the window of opportunity to visit family members inside the Caribbean basin. Being a British territory there was no need for a U.S. vise coming intransient to Grand Cayman Island. As the years unfold residing here in Cayman, I have met great minds of inquisitiveness for everything, except the gospel message. The Lord has also allowed me to serve on mission trips to Cuba and South Africa. The Apostle Paul in all his brilliancy came to a conclusion after his conversion. This is his testimony, *"I am determined not to know anything among you except Jesus Christ and Him crucified"* (1 Cor. 2:2).

In the book of Proverbs 13:20 we're cautioned about the type of company we keep. *"He that walketh with wise men shall be wise, but a companion of fools shall be destroyed."* As a child my Sunday school teachers taught me how to know my faith, own my faith and share my faith. I believe every person should know that the finished work on the Cross can save him/her from the wrath of God. The Son of God took my punishment for all my past, present and future sins. The only decision I had to make was that of accepting His offer of redemption.

King Solomon wrote, *"A wise man will hear"* (listen to the word of God) *"and increase learning"* (gain some form of education), *"and a man of understanding"* (ability to think rationally) *"will attain wise counsel"* (Prov. 1:5). Growing up did come with options. I choose to consider my ways and allow Jesus Christ to direct my course along life's journey. Every day He provides the opportunities, but I have to take them. Although my Salvation is sealed, I still have choices to make on an everyday basis.

Chapter Four

KNOW JESUS OR NO JESUS?

When the early pioneers of Christianity came to Siparia, I thought they came to stay permanently. Some like the Fairs and the Peters who came before the Penners knew how to adjust from cold to warmer climates. Except for the Penners, the other two couples had children who gradually adapted to our environment. Adapting to our lifestyle and cultural practices were part of the agenda expected on a field mission. Their first stage of transition was to secure a dwelling house in the neighborhood. The Trinidad mission board was instrumental in securing a dwelling house that will be used for future missionaries as the work progressed.

This house was close to my home on Mary Street, so their children became my friends. Not long after, they joined our friendly community through regular home visitations. This method also encouraged them to open their home and lives to new friends. Their rented house was built on posts (or stilts as some refer to them). This design allowed more space for a garage beneath the building. With two enclosing walls on the east and west sides, Reverend Peters transformed the garage into a sanctuary.

He was a handyman who blended into the carpentry trade with some of the other members of the church. They were family men like Brother Landor, Brother Halls, and Brother Nesbit who were no strangers to tools and skilled trades. On Saturday evenings, the garage became the meeting place for youth fellowship. Many "village boys and girls" found interest in the games and snacks that became part of the meeting. The devotional time with singing was enlightening to all who attended, especially when the Reverend's wife played the accordion.

On Wednesday nights after the Bible study, there was an hour of prayer time. Sometimes during the prayer, I would hear snoring coming from elderly folks. During the mango season, we listened for mangos dropping from the tree at the back of the building. There were also stray dogs on the street in front of the church building. Of course when the rain fell the water came gushing from the open entrance of the church down the sloped church floor. To top this list of distractions would be Reverend Peter's oldest son, Rodney, who sat with some children on the front bench.

With a short attention span, Rodney was heard chattering. He was cautioned first by his Dad's stern look. When that look failed, immediately after the service, he was taken to the back of the church. We heard crying afterwards. These are some of the memories that have become building blocks of the church that began under the house on Mary Street. The title was "The West Indies Mission" for several years. When the location changed, a new title was introduced: "The Siparia Evangelical Church." Nevertheless, the Lord continued increasing the attendance.

This was noticeable on the last Sunday night of each month. With a reel of film and a projector, Reverend Cross from the Arima Evangelical Church came to show us a biblical-based movie. The larger attendance created a need for more seating. Thanks to the skillful members, benches were made to extend the seating area. This increase continued as people from all over Siparia came out to fellowship. They wanted to know more about this Jesus we sang about. Those who envied our fellowship soon felt a desire to whole-heartedly join in the membership.

Christ died and rose as was prophesized. Therefore, the stone that was rolled away from the entrance of the tomb was not for Him to come out; but for us to see and believe. His authority over death completed the work He came to do. This event will be the final conclusion on Judgment day that determines the faith of every believer against the doubters. My mother used to remind me that people will know who I am by the friends I keep.

After several years of fellowshipping beneath the house on Mary Street, the day came when a vision was born: to move to a new location at the top of the hill about four hundred feet away.

This meant the members had to begin making monetary sacrifices towards their objective. The Lord blessed their faithfulness and in the fullness of time the land was purchased. With skillful resources within the membership, it was not long before work began on the site. This reality bought a new horizon for the community at the corner of Allies and Victoria Street. History was about to be written on the pages of our hearts. Saints who knew the Lord constantly bombarded His throne with petitions for material and finances to build this house of worship. Brother Halls was one of the few faithful members. He was employed with the British Petroleum oil company. He was able to get the ball rolling with donations from that company.

With other donations, the retaining wall, foundation, and other main structures were built by the members. The hilltop view took your eyes to the Southern Range. This spectacular view was first sighted in 1498 by Christopher Columbus. Upon completion, this building became a beacon for the surrounding neighborhood of Siparia. As one of the foundational members, I can testify to the Lord's generosity. This achievement was a giant step of faith, since the majority of members were not employed.

Worshipers from seven miles in proximity came to the church services. Some came walking, and others came cycling to both the day and night services. We all had in common the desire to learn more about this God the Bible refers to as the only True, Holy, and Just God. Only such a God can give His Son as ransom for an entire lost world. The doctrine on sanctification and justification was never preached at other religious gatherings in the district. Young and old with families were interested in the hope, faith, peace, and grace Jesus Christ offered without any strings attached.

However, when the transition began among the foreign missionaries, it had an effect that created vacant pews. This problem became the priority on the permanent member's prayer list. During this period, the Executive Church Board located in Arima shouldered the responsibility of shepherding the flock. They sent pastors from other churches to officiate on a rotation basis. On one occasion, they sent two single, dedicated female missionaries: Ms. Dona Williamson and Ms. Edith Johnson who were affiliated with the foreign mission board. They were assigned to Siparia congregation for a few years.

During which time they also got involved with church planting in the rural districts.

Their passion for church planting came with a simple method of creating cell groups in homes. As the groups developed, believers were encouraged to join the main body on the hilltop at Siparia. Those like Sinatra, Anderson, Frank and many more from the Morn Diablo house church came out to communion service once a month. This much-needed fresh inspiration for saints in Siparia came from other groups in Penal and Mendez villages. From those groups came believers with experience who eventually took leadership responsibilities in grooming others at those cell groups.

Before the ladies left the Siparia congregation, they recommended to the Executive Board three men for eldership duties. These men were to shoulder the leadership responsibilities until a full-time pastor arrived. It was Jesus who said, *"A prophet is not without honor except in his own country and in his own house"* (Matt. 13:57). Their remaining weeks were focused on counseling the newly elected elders. One of the many responsibilities of the elders was to begin a home visitation program among the believers attending. Those who were not as faithful in attendance became top priority.

There is a twofold blessing whenever the elders visited homes, especially those who were attendees. Like building bridges, it it requires a time for listening and a time for encouraging the people of God. The Christian faith has a "Chief Shepherd" who begins and finishes whatever He purposes to His glory. It is an assurance for all who put their trust in Christ. My response to serve as Elder was an answer to my prayers. At that stage of my journey, the Lord was teaching me about servanthood.

However, when special occasions like Christmas, Easter, weddings, and funeral services came around, a visiting pastor or the moderator for all the Evangelical Churches of the West Indies (E.C.W.I.) would come to preside. These events had no boundaries of limitations to the religious crowd who attended. Although some held on to their myths based on works, the message of salvation was preached at every occasion. Jesus, at one of His street meetings said, *"The cares of this world and the deceitfulness of riches choke out the Word."* One of several reasons why this continues among church goers today is *"due to a lack of understanding"* scripture (Matt. 13:18-22 with emphasis).

Every person who does not have the indwelling Holy Spirit of God feels or believes they can interrupt Holy Scripture without the aid of its Author. Before Jesus' death, He promised that He and the Father would send to his disciples "another helper." The Greek word for "helper" is *"parakletos."* It means a lawyer or assistant in a legal question. Someone who provides encouragement, counsel, and strength (Jn. 14:16; 15:26 16:7-15). The spirit's full ministry began on Pentecost. It marked the opening of the last ear of world history that will end when Christ returns (Acts 2:1-4).

Trinidad is a land over-flowing with many religious groups. However, Christians are still fortunate to worship in freedom. This freedom also stretches across the border for all other denominations, even to those who are echoing voices of antichrist gestures. It is difficult for the blindness of one's heart to accept or understand God's Son as the only propitiator.

As in days of old, today's world with ungodly leaders is trying to persuade young, confused minds. Those leaders publically express a vote of non-confidence towards the Son of God and His universal church. They are convincing un-churched folks to reject biblical truth as their foundational pillar in life. The Lord reminds His followers that *"Not even the gates of Hell will be able to prevail against it"* (it - as in the proclamation of the gospel message) (Matt. 16:18b with emphasis).

As a young boy, I had the choice of practicing the religion of my heritage. It was such that it said no to the doctrine of Jesus Christ. Its history is considered the antidote to delusions of omniscience. By God's grace after sixty-five years, I am still *"holding fast to the confession of my faith without wavering"* in Christ Jesus (Heb. 10:23 with emphasis). Getting to know the Savior is an experience of *"being led in the path of righteousness"* (Ps. 23:3b with emphasis). This is a way of life that can bring enmity with others who oppose the rule of theocracy.

The story of the three Jewish boys demonstrates great courage in refusing to bow down to an idol. From a polytheistic perspective, there was no god capable of delivering them. Yet they were obedient to the God of Abraham regardless of the consequences (Dan. 3:16-18). Here are a few promises when traveling through the valley of the shadow of death or other unpleasant circumstances: *"The Lord provides strength and peace to His people"* (Ps. 29:11 with emphasis).

"Whatever things were written before were written for our learning, that we (Christians) *through the patience and comfort of the scriptures might have hope"* (Rom. 15:4). Because of the *"resurrection of Jesus Christ we* (Christians) *have an inheritance that is incorruptible and undefiled that does not fade away which is in Heaven"* (1 Pet. 1:4 with emphasis). As a result of this assurance, I am comforted in body, soul, and mind as the spirit of God works in me.

Although I will not be perfect in experiencing the full blessings of the Lord on Earth, I would be a fool to say no to Jesus Christ and miss out on all these blessings and promises for all of eternity. During the first year of Jesus' ministry, He and His disciples went to Gergesenes. There he healed two men who were possessed by demons. It is interesting to learn that the demons *"begged Jesus"* not to send them back to where they belonged. Apparently the demons knew who this **"Jesus"** was and respected Him. It was not long after the whole city turned up to meet this **"Jesus."** However, what had just happened was of the least concern to them. Instead of rising to the occasion for the two men who were set free from demonic forces, they also *"begged"* Jesus to leave at once (Matt. 8:28-34). They saw a decline in their economy when a heard of swine ran into the water and drowned. In our modern world where the wheels of finance turn the hearts of many, I am not surprised when church goers are "begging" Jesus to leave them to their folly of deceitfulness.

It has become a global practice of some up-right citizens who are *"begging Jesus"* to get out of their educational institutes and not to enter their work places. Leaders who prefer Jesus and his followers to stay away from their sporting arenas, political band-wagons, and courts of justice. Religious worshipers who close their houses after attending a church service until the next weekly routine of greeting and hand shake all memorized. Is it because they fail to realized that the finished work on the Cross included our past, present, and future transgression?

The missionary, Jim Elliot, had these words to share before his death: *"He is no fool who gives that which he cannot keep to gain what he cannot lose."* Jim and other missionaries were massacred by 10

Waodoni warriors on January 8, 1956. The desire for a change of heart comes when a person seeks the Lord *"while He may be found"* and not on our terms (Isa. 55:6). The parable of the sower and the seed reveals the condition of a stubborn heart (Matt. 13:1-9). From the four types of hearts (or soil conditions), only one bore fruit. This was only possible with the aid of the Holy Spirit.

Although the responsibility was shared among those who watered, pruned, pulled weeds, fertilized, cropped, and guarded the plant; the fruit of life comes only from the breath of God. He spoke and it was so (Gen. 3:3-29). The Penners were seasoned workers who knew how to go after the lost sheep. Believers are admonished to *"let the word of Christ dwell in us richly in all wisdom so that we can teach and admonish each other"* (Col. 3:16 with emphasis). I saw them not as individuals with different nationalities. Their testimony identified that personal relationship with the Son of God. Such is a relationship that perpetuates your personality with peace and joy for all seasons of life. Knowledgeable as he was, Mr. Penner was humble enough to use his gifts and talents with anyone interested, especially young people. Reverend Penner served as Sunday school teacher, youth advisor, Pastor, husband, and father too many young people attending church. I cannot recall in all the years I've known him to be short-tempered, resentful, envious, boastful, self-centered, or timid. He spent his time attending to the people God placed in his care. With a song in his heart, and humor to share, there was never a dull moment when we were with him. I often wished they had come earlier when my brother Carlo was attending church.

With each visiting pastor that came before the Penners, I recall they all had that influential personality which challenged some of the older men and women. However, in the preceding years, Carlo's handsome masculine physique as a body builder eventually became his stumbling block. He and a few others began saying "no" instead of getting to "know" the Lord better. Under strange circumstances both Carlo and his friend Dolan, experienced tragic deaths. Dolan was employed at the Texaco Oil Company Refinery in Trinidad when he passed away on the job. Carlo, a former employee of Texaco, passed away in Saint Croix, U.S. Virgin Islands. He was employed with Hess Oil Refinery when his accident occurred.

Nevertheless, before more of the younger men left the church, the Lord spoke to Samuel and Ben about attending bible school. Their calling into the ministry came while fellowshipping at the new church building. With blessings from the local congregation and the Executive Board's assistance Ben was the first to leave. In the preceding years Samuel also left for Prairie Bible College in Alberta. Canada. After graduating only Samuel returned to take up his cross and follow the Lord. When my brother left the fellowship, some of my other siblings began attending occasionally. I saw this as an encouragement that could weave a thread of hope. But after a short season, their personal agendas became their priority.

This usually happens when we allow the deceitfulness of the world to choke out the Word of God. Nevertheless, I wanted to demonstrate to the world my allegiance to the Lord and His church. The short service at the water's edge of Mora Dam in 1970 was where Reverend Penner presided at my baptism. My desire to "know" more about Jesus Christ and His universal church became more intimate. The Psalmist said in Psalm 139:6, *"Such knowledge is too wonderful for me; it is high, I cannot attain to it."* One of Jesus' Apostles wrote in Acts 4:12, *"Salvation is found in no one else, for there is no other name under Heaven given to men by whom we must be saved."* A non-Christian historian named Will Durant said, *"The inversion of all political wisdom and of all sanity is echoed in Jesus' words He that is greatest among you, let him be your servant"* (Matt. 20:26). India's liberator, Mahatma Gandhi said, *"Jesus had lofty moral principles."* Many world-renowned officials have used quotes from Jesus Christ, yet very few have made time to get to know Him as their Lord and Savior.

The Jewish scholar, Joseph Klaussner wrote, *"It is universally admitted that Christ taught the purest and sublime ethics which throws the moral precepts and maxims of the wisest men of antiquity far into the shade."* These famous educators may have read the Bible from cover to cover, yet they lacked faith to trust Him on a personal basis. It took Jesus three days to change the world's concept on eternity. Now, twenty centuries later, no other human being is capable of setting a better precedent regarding life before and after death.

Moses was determined to remain without food and water for forty days and nights so that he could be in the presence of the most High

God. I am challenged not to complain when I'm out of my comfort zone. As a young man amidst uncomfortable circumstances, I was easily tempted to complain. When Moses descended to the crowd, they saw a radiant glow. No Israelites were able to gaze upon his face (2 Cor. 12:16). This begs the question: When I am in the presence of the unsaved, can they see the glory of God in me?

Born-again believers have the boldness to enter into His courts and get to know Him (Rom. 8:14). Did Mary know when she kissed her baby's face that she was kissing the face of God? (Matt. 1:18). Did Samson not get his final prayer request before dying? (Jude 16:28-29). Did not Thomas the (doubting) disciple became a faithful follower of the risen Christ? (Jn. 20:29). Faith my friend is *"the substance of things hoped for, the evidence of things not seen, without it, no one can please God. It comes by hearing the word of God"* (Heb. 11:1).

A Christian's journey is by faith, not by sight (Heb. 11:1 & 6). However, faith in the wrong person or thing can bring serious repercussion at the end of your life. It's like an assumption of confidence in a belief that has no substantial foundation of truth to rely on. In other words, I can say I know the current president of the United States. From undertaking research, I could give you a description of that person. I can go to great lengths to find out some of his personal interests. With a world of technology at my disposal, there is very little I'm not able to know about this person. But in all truth, this page of information does not give me the liberty to declare I know the President of America.

My dear friend, it is the same with knowing God. My personal efforts, my sacrifices, my commitments, and my will can be of purest devotions to God, but yet I don't know His beloved Son who died in my place. Without the personal knowledge of His Son, no one will be able to know God the Father.

It is why this journey reveals that *"in His presence is fullness of joy, at His right hand are pleasures forevermore"* (Ps. 16:11). The more I know the Word of God, the more I will become confident about my salvation (Jn. 17:3). Another responsibility the Penners took on during the camp seasons was becoming Mom and Dad to the youths. Seasonal camps were held at four venues; the locations included

Victory Heights in the north, Los-Iroes Beach in the south, Morugia in the east and Chagaramas in the west.

The E.C.W.I. executive body orchestrated the camping operations. They selected directors, counselors, speakers, and volunteers from all the churches on Island to assist with the weeks of camping. The enrollment was by age from all the district churches. Many came with a negative attitude saying no to Jesus Christ. However, when they left, it was with excitement to return to their home churches. The testimonies around the campfire spoke of genuine repentance and faith in accepting Christ as Lord and Savior. For many it usually came with tears of joy.

Attending camps had a lasting impact on me; especially with the new friends I made who were scattered across the island. I am grateful to the Lord for providing the type of environment where I was able to experience the pure joy of His Salvation without contamination. Here are the echoes of Pastor Thabiti Anyabwille, "*What I have as a sinner is the capacity to harm others because I lack the wisdom of God to do well. Sin warped my personality out of God's intended shape, so it will take a life time to be aligned.*" Perhaps some of these incidents that came to pass created doubts in the minds of un-churched folks. As a result, some continued to say no to Jesus Christ. Allow me to share a few thoughts worth considering.

I was not present when the Angel spoke to the disciples at the empty gravesite in the garden. I was not with those who walked with Him or sat at His feet listening to parables. I did not go sailing with the disciples and Jesus, nor did I witness Lazarus coming out of the grave. I was not present at His ascension in Bethany (Lk. 24:50-51). Those who saw Him also heard and wrote as eyewitnesses. Their testimonies of those He healed have shown physical proof of amazing miracles. Their testimonies have been authenticated by scholars of olden days. Centuries later, more stamps of approval are added to the authenticity of Holy Scriptures. Now available in several dialects, all people can know Him without excuses.

Jesus said this to His listeners, "*I and my Father are one; as the Father*" (God Almighty) "*knows me*" (Jesus Christ) "*even so I*" (Jesus Christ) "*know the Father*" (Jn. 10:15 & 30). Many religious followers claim to know God, but not all want to know His beloved Son. This truth is what separates Christianity as life to live, instead of a religion to practice. This is the backbone of evangelism. Without excuses, Christians are commanded to *"Go into the entire world and preach the Gospel"* beginning next-door (Matt. 28:18-19).

My first experience of engaging in evangelism was on a Sunday evening before service began. The Penners decided to take the young people' group on a street walk around the neighborhood. I was already intimidated by the thought of being seen with a Bible in my hand and walking to church. Now to add fear to intimidation, I had to speak to someone in my district about Jesus Christ. By the grace of God, the novelty of such a thought was replaced with confidence from 2 Timothy 3:16. It reminded me of the power of God's word for all circumstances in life.

I pay attention to the first word *"All"* of scripture. Not those in red letters, not those in the New Testament, and not only those in the Old Testament. *"All scripture is given by inspiration of God, and is profitable for doctrine, for reproof, for correction, for instruction in righteousness, that the man of God may be complete, thoroughly equipped for every good work."* I have to constantly guard against compromising the truth of the gospel message. When myths and theories are included in the gospel message, it favors the acceptance of the unsaved ears.

I grow weary of today's religionists who are leaving the waters of grace unruffled, to an envisaged fellowship with other gods. I have heard from the lips of the unsaved how some sermons can be boring and uncomfortable. I ask: Is not all of Scripture God's Breath? I have to constantly remind myself not to allow my faith to become mundane and routine. Many affluent societies prefer a worship service where traditions and cultural integration becomes the main focus of the sermon.

The pure essence of biblical truth is removed to accommodate bare, mortal literature. We have cunningly removed the authoritative word of God and settled for a simpler version of the Bible. Some translators have removed *"thus sayeth the Lord"* to misguide the unrepeated hearts. The believers are resting from the truth, while their surroundings struggle with turmoil. The Hindu religion questions the sovereignty of the Almighty God. They prefer a wider range of options where millions of gods become acceptable.

Another religion challenges the personified deity of Jesus Christ. They choose to believe in the encounter between a mortal man named Mohammed and the Angel Gabriel. At the same time, they live in denial that the same Angel Gabriel spoke to Joseph and Mary of Jerusalem (Matt. 1:20). We are blind if we worship the creature instead of the Creator (Rom. 1:25). Others reject the complete scripture as the divine revelation from God Almighty for a presentation from Joseph Smith and his encounter with an Angel called Maroni.

Another group of believers reject the Holy Bible as the final "Word" from the LORD (emphasis added). They choose to believe Ellyn White's rewriting of scripture as divine interoperating. The world is over-flowing with concepts that promise to supply all your heart's desires. However, no other doctrine declares these words from the Son of God, *"I am the way, the truth, and the life, no man comes to the Father, except through Me"* (Jn. 14:6). The apostle Paul reminded the saint at Ephesus, and believers today when he said, *"Let no one deceive you with empty words."* Why is such a reminder necessary? *"...Because of these things* {empty /vain / lies/} *the wrath of God comes upon the sons of disobedience, therefore do not be partakers with them"* (Eph. 5:6 & 7). As in days of old, the validity of Jesus Christ continues to puzzle many thinkers. It is a concern that comes under disguises with three deceptions. The first is through augments. The next shows off through debates. The third is often under the title of discussions. They all have one objective, to destroy the belief of the followers of Jesus Christ. The opponents of the cross will always have doubts, until they surrender their allegiance to the person who died on that cross.

He said to His followers, *"Let not your heart be troubled; you believe in God, believe also in Me"* (Jn. 14:1). He said this to the unbelieving followers, *"If you had known Me,* you *would have known My Father"* (Jn. 14:7). If only they had believed and obeyed the words of God. If I had kept a record of all my regrets, except for the grace of God, I would be still drowning in my miserable way of life. But the grace of God provides fresh opportunities from the day He saved me. We are known from birth by name and family identification. We grow to develop our own identity through character and personality. People recognize us by speech, action, and our physical appearance.

Then one day the big question comes, "Are you the son or daughter of so and so?" We often forget that we are image bearers of our parents and our Creator. Because we are so engulfed in a sinful world, it can become easy to lose the identity of a born-again believer. The words of Isaac Watts remind us that "*Not all the blood of beasts slain on Jewish altars could give the guilty conscience peace, or wash away sin. But Christ the heavenly lamb, takes all our sins away; a sacrifice of noble name and richer blood than they.*" Have you ever considered the fact that if God did not forgive, Heaven would be empty? Then He would not have said, "*I go to prepare a place for you- ...and I will come again to receive you*" (Jn. 14:2-5).

Every new day that daws upon mankind testifies to the handy works of a Creator much greater than His creation. As an outsider with no credentials to Roman authorities and Jewish hierarchy, Jesus spoke these words to the chosen apostles at His ascension, "*All authority has been given to Me in Heaven and on Earth*" (Matt. 18:18). When He came to Earth, His intention was never to command an army. He neither held a political office, nor owned property. He never had the need to invest in bonds and stocks, yet He owned the cattle on a thousand hills and the wealth in every land. He never invested in any financial institution, yet His wealth is seen in the Heavens.

Throughout history, His name has been the main focus in thousands of books around the world. Those who claim to have some type of encounter with the supernatural don't have any authority over death and the grave as He does. There are an overwhelming number of people who believe there is a God. They will boast of religious formalities they faithfully attend to. They believe their soul is secured. All of the above can happen without salvation in Jesus Christ. Therefore, my unsaved friend, without His salvation there is no guarantee to stand before Him to hear "*well done thou good and faithful servant.*"

As a religious follower, do not become gullible in believing God is limited to think like His creatures. Do not believe He has a soft spot for all, of how they have lived; that all will eventually get to

Heaven. If I choose to separate the Trinity of the God Head, then also separate from Holy Scripture. Any form of exclusion or addition to the Gospel message is a direct sin of blasphemes as warned in the book of Revelation (Rev. 22: 18 & 19). Whenever I remove one of the three components which comprise an egg, it will become less than its original purpose. Therefore, the conclusion of the matter is: a person cannot know God and reject His son.

Chapter Five

CHRISTIANS AMONG OTHER BELIEVERS

Every human being is a believer of some kind of doctrine or code of beliefs. One does not have to belong too, or be associated with, a religious denomination in order to be a believer. Man inherited a spirit which compels him to react with some type of reasoning. He has the capacity to communicate, regardless of the truth. However, if truth is to be examined for its validity, there must be something or someone to compare it with in order to reach a numinous decision.

Most societies with cultures and traditions have some type of religious activity. The act of worship began before the incarnation of the Christ of Bethlehem. Those who heard of the God of Adam, Moses, Abraham and the Jewish nation already had the first five books of the Old Testament. For Noah and his family, it was difficult but rewarding (Gen. 6:1-3). Their legacy of obedience has encouraged the Lord to bless others who worship Him in spirit and *"in truth"* (Jn. 8:32).

Untruth is the plague of sin that comes with the virus of rebellion among mockers of the cross. It will consume the heart with pride and cause blindness to the free gift of forgiveness available. When a person chooses to deny the Christian doctrine, it is usually for options which may be more conducive to their lifestyle. Some have fallen victim to manipulative teachings. As a result, their entrapment has embraced the cunningness of the web of lies. For those reasons *"the ungodly shall not stand in the judgment"* (Ps. 1:5 with emphasis).

They are compared in the above context to a dead and rootless plant. These persons like a puff of wind can be blown about by any doctrine that sounds good to them. Contrary to the hope and faith that is offered in the resurrection, a child of God is secured. *"For whom He foreknew, He also predestined to be conformed to the image of his*

Son" (Rom. 8:29). But to those who have no advocate, who will plead their case? The vehicle of religion encourages a good moral practice that infuses some degree of stability. It also manifests challenging objectives with great accomplishments. People who walk that path often don't see the need for the gift of salvation.

On the contrary are the believers who may not be materially successful, but become grateful for the joy of their salvation. Their faithfulness outweighs the success in theology, philosophy, and science. With Jesus Christ as the author of the Christian faith, why not join in and become part of His universal church? (Matt. 16:18). This is another of His promises, "YOU- God- will keep him in perfect peace whose mind is stayed on YOU" (Isa. 26:3). Those who are looking for "short-cuts" to get to God will someday hear, "Depart from Me, I never knew you" (Matt. 7:23).

When the spirit of the Lord calls a person into a personal relationship, remember that person was before "dead in trespasses and sins" (Eph. 2:1). Attending funerals as a young man was never something I looked forward too. The topic of death is feared and uncomfortable for many people. It gives the tendency of feeling separated for eternity. Without knowledge based on the doctrine of salvation in Jesus Christ, there is no other hope beyond the grave.

One day Jesus attended a funeral. It was in the town of Bethany where Mary lived. Her sister, Martha, and brother, Lazarus, were also close friends of Jesus. Nevertheless, He was summoned immediately due to Lazarus' illness (Lk. 11:38). Jesus providentially knowing the present and future of all circumstances, decided to arrive four days later (Jn. 11:32). His disciples joined Him in meeting the grumbling crowd. Many of them failed to realize His authority over all of creation. I also stand guilty at times for lack of faith in His full authority over our deteriorating world. I am so glad that "His thoughts are not like (my) thoughts, nor are His ways like (mines)" (Isa. 55:8 with emphasis).

In spite of religious beliefs and other confusing thoughts, this is what God thinks every time one of His children dies, "Precious in the sight of the Lord is the death of his saints" (Ps. 116:15). As the grieving hearts looked to Jesus, He gave instruction to remove the grave cover. Silence was broken as He echoed the words "Lazarus, come forth!" Only the few who remembered the teaching from the book of Isaiah in 55:11 watched in faith as they gazed at the grave. *"So shall My words be that goes forth from my mouth; it shall not return unto me void, but it shall accomplish what I please, and it shall prosper in the thing for which I sent it."* Perhaps if he had just said, *"Come forth"* several others would have come out of their graves that day.

The Christian faith is a personal relationship between each sinner and the Holy God. It comes only through the justification of His Son (Heb. 3:7-8). *"In Him is the light of life."* There have been times when I felt like those sisters. I wondered if Jesus had forgotten me and why my prayer requests hadn't been answered. Those are the moments when my faith seems limited. It happens when hope is exhausted by *"the sting of death"* (1 Cor. 15:56). The waiting period becomes unbearable; sometimes doubt and fear turns into unnecessary weeping. Friends and family who don't know Jesus will always doubt, like the crowd at the gravesite. But, if we trust in the Lord with all our heart, He promises never to forsake us.

Gone are the years when my father would become indifferent in understanding why I wanted to attend church services as a boy. To *"keep myself unspotted from the world,"* I felt church fellowship would keep me focused (Jam. 1:27 with emphasis). Many times I am faced with this rhetorical question: *"Is my lifestyle lacking the integrity of a Christian?"* All Christians are given various measures of faith to encourage the body of believers. Each believer is also given gifts which are different to the talents they are born with. These gifts are for building and edifying not for personal fame or gain. We use them to support those who are susceptible to failures when drawn away by enticing lust and cravings (Jam. 4:1; Rom. 12:3 & 6).

Let us now consider this interesting Parable of the Wheat and the Tare recorded in Matthew 13:24-30 by the "Chief Shepherd." It is meant to alert the conscience of leaders and shepherds in His vineyard. The assumption of incompetence by the caretakers in this narrative is mentioned in verse twenty-five, *"While men slept the enemy came."* Apparently, the culprits infiltrated under camouflage, and came to destroy with deceitfulness in mind. The integrity of the servants stumbles due to unfaithfulness. They were sleeping instead of waking and guarding the field. The Lord of the Harvest continues to warn His caretakers, shepherds, deacons, elders, pastors and overseers (to name a few) who are entrusted with the same responsibility for guarding "the flock of God." I am equally guilty when excuses appease my selfish nature to prevent fellowshipping with the saints. Although Jesus rested during his long journeys, He used those times to refresh His followers.

He kept focused and was never found lacking in self-discipline. My prayer is never to become comfortable using this phase as an excuse, *"The spirit indeed is willing but the flesh is weak"* (Matt. 26:41b). Now climb with me to "the Mount of Olives" where the serene beauty of Gethsemane exposes Jesus' choice of spending his last night together with His disciples (Matt. 26:36-47). Let's capture a polarized view of the coming activities prior to His death. It would be safe to assume that they were equally strenuous after the hectic day of evangelism in the town of Jerusalem.

The Master took His co-laborers to this place with the intention of spending that night in prayer. Weary bodies and fatigued minds made it difficult to focus on His agenda. Their thoughts of what will happen tomorrow were easily vanished from their weary minds. Previously Jesus kept reminding them of His death and resurrection. However, that evening they were in no mood for praying. I can relate to similar instances as a young Christian attending Wednesday night prayer meetings.

There were folks at the service who felt they had to tell the Lord all their gossiping tales of the week. Talk about "praying without ceasing." It was more like sleeping without praying for me. Back at the garden, the surrounding atmosphere echoed the hounding of chilled breezes upon the moon-lit hilltop. The pounding of His heartbeat vibrated the emotional stress with deep loving concerns for all of humanity. The knowledge of His Father's full wrath and the catastrophic results of the crucifixion were not a task for any mortal to bear.

His body began to experience a rare medical condition called "hematohydrosis." This is when the capillary blood vessels that feed the sweat glands rupture, causing them to release blood instead of water. However, most of those "pain-staking" hours in prayer went unnoticed. The weary disciples slumbered and slept as the Good Shepherd kept watch. They saw Him dripping with blood as a ray of moonbeam struck upon His weary back. In kneeling posture, He began to intercede on my behalf and yours, dear friend.

What type of man is this? What type of prophet is this? What type of teacher or philosopher is this that the God of all Creation would send to fulfill His perfect plan of salvation? From the scrolls of the prophet Isaiah come these sobering thoughts recorded in 53:4 -5:

> *Surely He has borne our grief, and carried our sorrows; yet we esteemed him stricken, smitten by God, and afflicted. But he was wounded for our transgressions, He was bruised for our iniquities, the chastisement for our peace was upon him. And by his stripes we are healed.*

I wondered if this human thought ever crossed His mind that night: *"Can "I" (Jesus) depend of these disciples to continue sowing seeds for the Kingdom of My Father when I'm gone?"* In the same context I have to ask myself, *"What are my excuses for sleeping and not praying?"* Matthew takes up this broken puzzle and continues to share his views from various angles, hoping that we would grasp the seriousness of this dramatic scene in the unfolding story of a leader among leaders.

He adds a different twist to the previous disciple's comments; yet for all intents and purposes we notice how man's frailty collapses under emotional feelings and formalism. At this point in time, the luxury of their necessities became a stumbling block. In the following months and years ahead, each of them in various ways along their missionary journeys, will be refreshingly reminded of the intensity of that painful night Jesus spent alone praying while they slept. I sometimes wonder, *"Is the church still sleeping today?"*

Have we grown weary in waiting for our Lord's return (while the harvest is ripe)? When will believers be awakened to take their responsibility as faithful disciples? Christians are admonished to *"watch and pray"* especially in an age like ours. The apostle reminds each believer in Christ that *"we do not wrestle against flesh and blood"* (Eph. 6:12a). In his first epistle to the elders shepherding the flock in churches scattered across Asia, Peter wrote, *"Be sober, be vigilant"* (1 Peter 5:8). Why was this necessary when many thought that Christ would soon return? Why was there this type of admonition to sojourning pilgrims? He continued, *"Because your adversary, who is the Devil walks about like a roaring lion, seeking who he may devour."* To be steadfast in the faith is a virtue much to be harvested from the gift of patience, dear weary soldier of the Cross. Every faithful shepherd who "labors" for this Master, should pay particular attention (even with his life) in guarding the fold of the redeemed. He should be skillful and competent in handling the sword of the spirit (which is the word of God).

Faithful shepherds get involved with perseverance and supplication for all the saints entrusted to them. Paul the Apostle reminds believers again in Ephesians 6:17-18 to be obedient and put on the armor of God. This armor allows us to fight against the *"wiles of the devil"* (Eph. 6:11). Fallen humans are no match for the evil one, so Christ equips the saints with the Holy Spirit and the full armor of God. It took me a while to understand that this full armor of God is the complete revelation of His Word (not the words of mortal man).

I hope my unsaved friends will recognize how weak, helpless, and defenseless they are on their own strength. The agony of defeat has entangled humanity when sin disrupted perfection and holiness in the Garden. The Bible declares in Rom. 5:6 that, *"For when we were yet without strength, in due time Christ died for* (us) *the ungodly."* Therefore, believers have to constantly depend on the Holy Spirit for the thrill of victory.

"And this is the victory that has overcome the world" (1 Jn. 5:4b). Thanks to photography, those of us who are not privileged to travel around the world can still see the majestic beauty of creation and the innovations man has achieved over the centuries. Our movie media now brings us a microscopic view into the once forbidden areas of secrets never before seen. With this science, I can see the fields where both wheat and tares grow together. The subtle difference in similarity can be difficult to recognize with normal eyes.

It is the reason Jesus advises the reapers to allow these plants to reach full maturity before harvesting (Matt. 7:17-19). As a young believer, I paid attention to older religious followers. Walk if you will for a while with me; share my thoughts on a familiar situation. Sometimes your friends may ask an embarrassing question regarding a member of your congregation. Because of the nature of the question, and what it conveys, you are caught speechless. You hesitate due to the wide range of assumptions.

With a stunned and curious tone of voice, you will probably ask, why? (Chances are you may know such a person.) However, I am not comfortable to be questioned by an unsaved person about my brothers or sisters in Christ. Nevertheless, since Christians are not perfect (yet), I have to listen and reply with honesty not compromising the truth. Christians often forget that the unsaved friends around them are constantly examining their life style. Jesus lived an exemplified life-style in spite of the hostile environment. Pastor John Piper at the "Together for the Gospel" (T4G -08) conference said, "*Jesus did not defend the free-will system.*" Pastor Mark Denver at that same conference said, "*Christians are different to other believers, due to the gospel-centered life that comes from within.*" The world will not see Jesus right now. However, they will see you and me.

All who propagate the cause of Christ here on Earth will be judged by unsaved spectators. Their objective is to look for differences between Christians and other believers. They are searching for the truth Christ offers to us. They already know the lies from Satan. Jesus taught His disciples the ethics of the kingdom of God. He said to them, "*Beware of false prophets who come to you in sheep's clothing*" (Matt. 7:15). Sometimes it is more difficult to recognize them among the church gathering. But Jesus said, "*You shall know the tree by its fruit*" (Matt. 7:20).

"*The very essence of Christianity produces something explicitly different to the world's standards for which skeptics realize, even if they refuse to accept the full truth of the Gospel. Is it now time for born-again Christians to advocate for the integrity of our (new) character?*" (Pastor Thabiti Anyabwile). Listening to conversations of the average Sunday morning cosmopolitan church-goers, they assume everyone (all religious organizations) is part and parcel of the family of God. This tells me, that their schooling about salvation, Jesus Christ and eternity is not of major importance.

Here is the instruction Paul left young Timothy in his first epistle chapter 6:3. He said, "*If any man teach otherwise and consent not to wholesome words, even the word of our Lord Jesus Christ, and to the doctrine which accords with Godliness, he is proud, knowing nothing.*" Prior to this statement, Paul warns Timothy of such teachers in chapter 4:2. They are *"proud, speaking lies in hypocrisy having their conscience seared with a hot iron."*

I have to be aware of sermons about a black cow, eating green grass, giving white milk and having red meat, instead of the "gospel message." New religions evolve when we throw all these ideas into the melting pot of fallen human standards. They defy the principles of pure Christianity. When you die, and stand before the Lord God of all creation. He asks of you, "Why should I (Almighty God) let you (a sinner) into My Heaven?" What would be your answer? The Bible teaches that there is only one way to enter Heaven.

If you are involved with some other form of religious organization that has presented other ways to enter Heaven, let me strongly suggest that you get out "A. S. A. P." (as soon as possible). Pause for a moment and allow the echoing of this solitary, sobering thought infuse your mind with these words written by the prophet in 1 Sam. 15:22. *"To obey is better than sacrifice."* It is true that our troubled perplexing societies need a new radical system, something that will stimulate a purpose for existence and bring about happiness.

Some believe this will eventually come with much sacrifice. Be it spiritual, mental, or physical, it can be an accomplishment with a turnabout to life like an insurance policy. However, the ultimate question will be: What happens after physical death? Religious followers like the Pharisee were known to enter a plea bargaining for selfish gains. The arranged sentencing of Jesus was one that caused their plan to backfire that resurrection morning. So too did the plan of Judas, before he hung with remorseful guilt outside the city of Jerusalem (Matt. 27:3-8).

The people said no to Jesus when they could not get what they wanted from Him. As long as Jesus fed them and healed them, they were willing to follow Him. That tendency of selfish greed continues among some churchgoers today. As long as my family and I are prospering, Jesus is okay for now. Jesus hung with compassion and mercy so the price of my sin was paid in full. Sin is diagnosed as *"a universal deformity of human nature, found at every point in every person. It is the energy of irrational, negative and rebellious reaction towards God.*

It is a spirit of fighting God to play God." (J.I Packer, Concise Theology.) Romans 3:9-23 and 1 John 1:8-10 give us these doctrinal explanations. In Psalm 51, we have a confession from King David. It occurred after the Prophet Nathan spoke to him regarding his adultery and murder. Then with a condemned heart, he cries out for God's mercy in repentance. His final words to the Lord were, "*Do not take Your Holy Spirit from me.*" Sin has the tendency of rebelling against God's rule. It has become part of human nature whenever we think, speak, and act contrary to His Holy nature. Therefore, we have lost all ability for any spiritual good. Scripture has had two distinct statements echoing throughout every generation since the dawn of time.

Both are described in Romans 3:10 & 23: "*As it is written, there is none righteous, no, not one. For all have sinned and fall short of the glory of God.*" Look with me beyond the leaves, come past the branches, and let's move away from the clustered trees. Join me in the greener pastures where the lamb and the lion will cuddle together some day. It is where mortality will be robed with His righteousness. It is where all sanctified nations will resume their God-given privileges and position among the Cherubs and Immortals. All who know Him as, "*the Alpha and the Omega*" will spend eternity with Him (Rev. 22:13).

There are different schools of doctrine regarding eternity. One falsifies "paradise" as a place of pleasurable sensuality. Another carries the concept that Jesus with his wife and children reside on another celestial planet beyond the galaxies. Access to that planet comes only from the "mortal man" who spoke to the Angel Maroni. Then again there are those who prefer to believe that they will remain in a state of extra-terrestrial existence after they die. Compare these and more to what you are about to read from an eyewitness.

The eyewitness was John, an apostle of Christ. In one of his narrations, a question is poised at Jesus regarding His whereabouts after His death (Jn. 14:1-4). Although they spent about three and a half years with the Son of God, it appeared none of them really got to know Him as he anticipated. Witnesses told us that He ate, slept, talked, walked, wept, got angry, did miracles, and exercised power of the elements of nature in their presence.

He did what was humanly impossible and practiced an average. Jewish lifestyle that at times it was difficult to identify Him among a small crowd. For all intent and purposes He repeatedly tried to refresh their minds about the details of His mission. Yet John tells us they somehow became complacent and disregarded the teachings about His mysterious death, burial, and resurrection. Even when He announced these sobering words, "*I go to prepare a place for you, I will come again,*" they were hearing but not listening. Perhaps they were used to the government officials propagating similar promises but never fulfilling them.

It was the great Mahatma Gandhi that said, "*I shall say to the Hindus that your lives will be incomplete unless you reverently study the teachings of Jesus.*" Did he notice a difference between Christians and other believers? The Muslims are taught, "*No bearer of a burden can bear the burden of another.*" Yet Christ did bear the cross for sinners (Surahs 17:15; 35; 18, Ali & Hingorani 23). Humans cannot escape the cascading reality of death, and at the same time search for ways to escape eternal punishment.

My unsaved friend, be wiser than the Pharisees and receive redemption before approaching the entrance of death (Lk. 23:40–43). His salvation knows no boundary or respect of persons. One day, Jesus addressed a curious crowd in the city and said, "*Come unto Me, all you who are labor and heavy laden, and I will give you rest; take my yoke upon you and learn from Me, for I am gentle, and lowly in heart, and you will find fest for your souls; for My yoke is easy and My burden is light*" (Matt. 11:28-30).

Some believed, but the scoffers walked away and perished. Many are still asking, what has the cross saved me from? I pray your answer will be able to justify the reason for Christ going to the cross. In his book, "The Cross-Centered Life," Pastor C.J. Mahaney said, "*It brought transformation to all who believe.*" I have to be mindful not to follow Christ for personal gains.

I must attend to scripture, rather than worldly gossiping. "*For I say unto you, that except your righteousness shall exceed the righteousness of the Scribes and Pharisees, ye shall in no case enter into the kingdom of Heaven*" (Matt. 50:20). Also, "*The distinctiveness of a Christian character exhibits faith and works coherent to different objectives perused by the religionist"* (Pastor Thabiti Anyabwile).

Jesus continues His teaching as Matthew dictates in chapter 16:26b, *"What shall a man give in exchange for his soul?"* Observe how He emphasizes the value of a soul compared to all of His other creations. Though all were created perfectly, only man will be responsible for his soul's final destination. We are not created like robots or androids that have to be pre-set or programmed to function. The Lord God gave "humans" the free will of choice with an eternal soul (Gen. 2:7).

What was near and dear to me as a young teen has now been placed in a different context of value? With maturity there are changes in values to things worth holding on to for a while. The aging process has been kind by allowing me to downsize as my activities begins to slow me down. However, some things are priceless namely, every human being. I know God has created people who do not have a deprecation value, not even our worst enemy.

After stepping into the rings of matrimony, my responsibilities increased causing a review on my wants and my needs. It took a while for me to determine if my "wants" were truly my "needs." When my priorities were in accordance with our objectives, the easier our journey became as husband and wife. The Lord still continues to remind me after forty years of togetherness that *"it's a learning process to prioritize our wants so they turn into needs, because we can become venerable to this fleshly craving if left unattended"* (Pastor Thabiti Anyabwile).

The Bible gives us a hint regarding valuable possessions. One of which we cannot use as a trade off on Judgment Day. Jesus asked a crowd of followers *"What will a man give in exchange for his soul?"* (Matt. 16:26). Years later, the Apostle Paul writing to the saints in Rome urged them to avoid divisive persons who cause divisions in the church. He said, *"I beseech you, brethren, mark them which cause divisions and offences contrary to the doctrine which ye have learned, and avoid them."* Don't make conversation, don't try to reason or give explanation, just avoid them and of course pray for them.

Paul went on to say, *"For they that are such serve not our Lord Jesus Christ, but their own belly, and by good works and fair speeches deceive the hearts of the simple"* (Rom. 16:17-18). These would be "churchgoers" who fabricate fables in presenting the gospel message. The writer of Proverbs 17:4 said, *"An evildoer gives heed to false lips, a liar listens eagerly to a spiteful tongue."* Paul took Christianity to the cradle of the gentile nations preaching and teaching whatever Jesus commanded him and not his Jewish religion (Matt. 28:19).

"The world sees Christians as users of Jesus to get the similar things they have by doing what others do, but not what Christ wants us to do" as voiced by Pastor John Piper. However, the Psalmist did remind us that, *"The Lord taketh pleasure in them that fear Him, in those that hope in His mercy"* (Ps. 147:11).

It was Jesus who said, *"Come now, and let us reason together"* (Isa. 1:18). Remember He is the God of Omniscience to whom you should be reasoning with. The subtle difference between Christianity and other religions is the difference between facts and fiction. A foundation of truth does not depend upon assumptions for its support. Neither should any born-again believer have to depend upon favorable circumstances to follow Christ. When I consider how His mercy and grace have brought more blessings to me and my extended home circle, I have no need to choose any other deity. Those who have exhausted their living chasing after worldly pleasures are now growing weary with stressful aging.

The emotional stress of a guilty conscience of a rebellious heart is what Christ came to set at peace. Those who fail to acknowledge His offer should know that *"Hell and destruction are before the Lord, how much more than the hearts of the children of men?"* (Prov. 15:11). The Bible tells us *"It is not the desire of the Lord for any to perish."* The Prophet Isaiah writes in chapter 1:18, *"Though your sins be as scarlet,* (not black as some refer to) *they shall be as white as snow, though they be red like crimson, they shall be as wool."* His unconditional love can reach the very least of sinners because He reached me.

When a person struggles alone, they often have a difficult time getting a true perspective of their problems. *"Plans fail for lack of counsel, but with many advisers they succeed"* (Prov. 15:22). I recall many decisions that brought detestable consequences. It was due to lack of counseling. As a young believer, some of the wrong perceptions imbedded in my heart could have been avoided. If only I had listened to advice and accepted instruction which scripture offered me (Prov. 19:20).

Many live in isolation; lonely and rejected from friends and family. I can assure all of God's love and eternal provision He demonstrated this on the Cross. Other leaders of religions and cults may be convincing with persuasive words; but God's words do not return unto Him void. In the various schools of thought based on spiritual beliefs, there is always some mandatory form of effort inclusive in an attempt of "knowing" that god. Only in the Christian faith are there provisions made. It occurred in the Garden of Eden when man disobeyed God (Gen. 3:15).

Forty days after His resurrection, Jesus appeared and fellowshipped with His disciples before His bodily ascension. What happened after Mohammed died? What happened after Braham died? What happened after Elin White died? What happened after Joseph Smith died? What happened after Buddha died? What happened after your mortal spiritual leader died? The testimony of two men leaving Jerusalem after the resurrection is recorded in Luke 24:13-30. Their conversation while walking to the village of Emmaus is worth considering. There are occasions with today Christian's when their conversation with Jesus sounds familiar.

However, after Pentecost, believers became bolder and began preaching in the open (Acts 2:1-21). The Holy Spirit reminds us that "He that which hath begun a good work in you will perform it till the day of Jesus Christ" (Phil. 1:6 with emphasis). Every believer from that day is equipped with "gifts" to proclaim the gospel message and build His church. The Lord speaking through King Solomon had this to say: "There is a way that seemeth right to a man, but its end is the way of death" (Prov. 14:12). Jesus said, "The way of a fool is right in his own way" (Prov. 12:15). Confusion, anger, and at times depression come when "a double minded man is unstable in all his ways" (Jam. 1:8).

God is still searching for sinners with these words: "Let the wicked forsake his way, let him return to the Lord." This announcement of assurance is valid and real as the air you now breathe (Isa. 55:7). In the Christian faith, it is "God who hath not given us the spirit of fear, *but of power, and of love, and of a sound mind"* (2 Tim. 1:7). History recalls the famous Thomas Edison who was afraid of the dark. As a result, he did something about it that has benefitted mankind since then. Electricity is the most in-demand of all other inventions in the modern world. We rely on it to assist in life and death. Yet it cannot sustain life <u>after</u> death.

These are the electrifying words from the Son of God *"I am the light of the world; he who follows Me shall not walk in darkness, but will have the light of life"* (Jn. 8:12). He supplies spiritual light in our dark world and eternal light in Heaven; two for the price of one sacrifice. If you can walk a while with these thoughts from King Solomon and ponder the essentials of them, you will find a resting place for your soul. He said, *"To everything there is a season, a time for every purpose under Heaven"* (Ecc. 3:1-8). Then, after trying every imaginary thing under the sun, Solomon came to this conclusion, *"God will bring every work into judgment, including every secret thing, whether good or evil'* (Ecc. 12:14). Wow! It really doesn't give anyone room for excuses, does it? Therefore, the fact of the matter is; what would be my final outcome on the road I choose to journey until I die? As a follower of Christ I choose to believe these words from the Psalmist, *"I have been young, and now old; yet have I have not seen the righteous forsaken, nor his seed begging bread"* (Ps. 37:25).

Christians should realize the difference between the cost of living, and their living that is costing too much. Sometimes, going after name brands can contribute to unnecessary stress, fatigue and worry. The unsaved and their "silent gods" fail to realize *"it is not possible that the blood of bulls and goats could take away sins"* (Heb. 10:4). Nor does the God of the Holy Bible require *"sacrifices and offering, burnt offerings and offerings for sin."* It is not His desire to obtain pleasure from them (Heb. 10 8).

The polytheistic deities from the wide range of religions, cultures and mythologies scattered across the world usually ascribes good over evil; their teachings aspire all things to all people with some degree of limitations. However, they provide no concrete evidence of living with the Creator after physical death. This is why Christianity begs the question to the followers of the above. Which of your "gods" have returned from the dead to begin the process of consummation? Matthew a disciple and writer pens these farewell words as Jesus ascends to Heaven in chapter 28:18: *"I am with you always, even to the end of the age."* Then these are from Him in Heaven recorded by John the disciple in the book of Revelation 22:12. *"And behold, I am coming quickly, and My reward is with Me, to give to everyone according to his work."*

His supreme power and authority over all of creation makes it possible to provide Salvation for every single person who asks. This Salvation comes after the forgiveness of all my sins. It entails my present, my past and the future sins in the rebirth process. He said, *"Where sin increased, grace increased all the more. So that just as sin reigned in death, so also grace might reign through righteousness to bring eternal life through Jesus Christ our Lord"* (Rom. 5:20b & 21).

A famous songwriter penned these words after his conversion. *"Years I spent in vanity and sin, caring not that my Lord was crucified."* I thank the Lord He did not allow me to spend years in vanity before I found out that, *"Happiness does not consist in the abundance of things"* (Lk. 12:15). Many folks do not agree with that statement. They have proof that money can buy everything, including love and security. (Perhaps with the Trademark-Hell bound.) Here are two proverbial expressions worth considering, *"A wise man will hear, and will increase learning, and a man of understanding shall attain unto wise counsels. Doth not wisdom cry and understanding put forth her voice?"* (Prov. 1:5 & 8:1).

Instead of man getting to the root of his problems, he tries to solve them with an overdose of excuses and self-pity Band-Aids. Pastor Thabiti Anyabwile puts it this way, *"Often we try to rationalize sin, and thereby go deeper into evil."* The Lord Jesus Christ said in Matthew's gospel, chapter 11:28, *"Come unto me, all ye that labor and are heavy laden, and I will give you rest."* This statement has never been declared by any other religious leader.

No mortal man dared to make such a claim or has been able to fulfill such promises. Throughout scripture we read, *"And it came to pass."* Prophecies by His mercies are daily coming to pass. The final pages of history are being revealed across the world, as the weakness of the heart opens to hate and anger against others. Every day a Christian looks in the mirror and sees the reflection of His image. Creation reveals His glory to the ungodly as they continue to destroy it. His Word is not frozen in time, nor should they be like recitations or accepted as myths from human analogies.

A Christian's spiritual growth should not be determined by an ecumenical congregation curriculum. Because, *"there is one God, and one mediator, between God and man, the man Christ Jesus"* every born again has direct access to Almighty God. I do not need the Pope or Mother Mary to speak on my behalf. Nor is Dr. Billy Graham in any authority to represent me on judgment day. With due respect, no mortal king or queen can do what has already been done by the Son of God on our behalf (1 Tim. 2:5).

The book of Hebrews reminds us that, *"We* (Christians) *have not a high priest which cannot be touched with the feeling of our infirmities"* (Heb. 4:15). Therefore, we should, *"Trust in the Lord with all our heart,* (not halfhearted) *and lean not unto our own* (academic) *understanding in all our ways* (every imaginary thought) *acknowledge Him, and He shall direct our paths"* (Prov. 3:5-6). My old Sunday school song comes to mind: *"Read your Bible, pray every day, and you will grow, grow, and grow."*

Pastor John Mac-Arthur reminded his listeners that, *"Soft preaching makes hard people, and hard preaching makes soft people." "The worship among Christians should be infested with the beauty of Holiness because evil is subjected in the presence of Holiness,"* (Pastor Thabiti Anyabwile). A sample of this truth is recorded for us in the gospel of Mark 1:21-24. The question from the two demons in Gergesenes was: *"What have we to do with You, Jesus, You son of God?"* (Matt. 8:28-32).

Even demons believe in God (James 2:19) because *"God is angry with the wicked every day"* (Ps. 7:11). The apostles cautioned the saints about deceivers who mingle with apostasy.

Paul, writing to the young believers at Thessalonica said, *"Let no man deceive you by any means* (2 Thess. 2:2-4). I remember as a boy how it felt to be deceived by people I trusted. The bitter emotional hurt came not at the time of deception, but after. I had to live with it for the rest of my life. Although forgiveness was granted, you will remember the fall. It's like Jesus getting scares on His body, especially where the nails punched his hands and feet. They remained after His resurrection to remind us of the price paid to redeem all sinners.

I can't imagine the torment; pain and guilt a non-believer will have to live with for all eternity. They will be constantly reminded of their wrong choice to reject Jesus Christ as their Lord and Savior. Deception always has a price, ask Adam and Eve. My cousin Timothy from Houston often keeps in touch with me via e-mail. He often includes these lines in red letters, *"I have been thinking, if Heaven is not true, what I lose? Nothing. But what if it is, and I didn't get ready? Then I would lose everything. What do you think?"*

Chapter Six

GIVE THE GIFT FOR LIFE

Whenever the word 'gift' is mentioned in my immediate family, an over-whelming sense of anxiety is visible. Regardless of the size, shape, color, or weight, receiving gifts has always been appreciated. As a child, receiving and giving gifts at Christmas seemed to complete the manger memories of the advent season. As the years passed, circumstances shifted to financial priorities and my anticipation was not as heart throbbing as before.

Nevertheless, the exchanging of gifts for various occasions continues to integrate our annual calendar. For every culture, there are different schools of thought on this subject of giving gifts. There are some religious denominations that exclude this practice of giving collectively, while some individuals tend to receive graciously. Nevertheless, when giving a token for appreciation, consideration is taken into account of the recipient's personality and character.

Giving gifts in my family often include some form of celebration. It is why some guidelines help in giving the element of surprise. With the growing of my own family, some gifts depreciated while others tended to increase with priceless memories. If you had similar experiences of shuffling your calendar dates to fit your finances, then join me in believing that age brings reasoning to these occasions.

Gift giving has been adopted from our extended families in Trinidad. Regardless of religious beliefs or cultural differences, the universal language of smiles enhances the opportune moments in time. Every year the list grows longer with new faces that fluctuate in moods and ages. My wife and I often have to reconsider its cost and do a quality control to make the necessary accommodations. This practice helps to avoid stressful repercussions and last minute mistakes. Acquiring gifts can be a pleasurable task for some; however, I have had my moments of weariness among the family shoppers.

It has been voiced that, "*A thing of beauty is a life-time of happiness.*" Things may last for a while, but I prefer to believe true beauty comes from within. From ancient traditions, this concept brings to light the important values which bind the hearts of many people scattered across our frontiers. Beaming from the ancient Holy Land is the dawning of the Nativity celebration. This became favorable for Christians with a decree from Pope Julius in 350 AD. In the preceding years, this act of benevolence has engulfed commercial enterprises with a different objective.

Nevertheless, the Bible and other literary books of merit have kept the essence of "gift giving" alive. Contrary to popular beliefs, its terminology has been misused at times for devious reasons. Many have felt the load of stress instead of the joy and peace given at that first Bethlehem occasion. The world has changed, so too have traditions and cultures. With regards to the gift God gave to humanity, very few are concerned. Many worshipers have **not** allowed the Baby Jesus to grow up and become their Lord and Savior. He remains their sweet baby Jesus all year round, while others have left Him hanging on the cross.

Giving gifts conveys a wide range of values. Depending on your options, from simplicity to extravagant the concept of "demand and supply" is never limited. The two main thoughts I hope to convey when giving gifts are that of goodwill and love. Its hidden manifesto is never without a high price tag to desperate shoppers. For the next consideration on the topic of gift giving, allow me to introduce another valuable type of gift. It carries its weight in liquid, while its worth is priceless. It is given freely to friends and foes without hesitation when in demand.

While some sacrificially give it, those who receive it are favored with some form of life support. The dramatic movie, *Seven Pounds,* with the main character portrayed by Mr. Will Smith is a story which allows viewers to contemplate the gift for life. Circumstances surrounding an incident draw him into a state of unrest; therefore, he attempts to gain his personal "redemption" by donating some of his own body parts. Each of the seven recipients contacted was grateful for the opportunity to continue with their lives more comfortably. However, Mr. Smith's haunting guilt eventually drove him to a suicide mission. He blamed himself for the death of his family while he was driving the vehicle that crashed and killed them.

The audience commends him for such a heroic deed in giving those gifts for life. Saddened by his choice of escape, I assumed he never found eternal peace. By ending his life, Mr. Smith apparently disregarded what the Creator allowed him to keep. His choice of early death felt it necessary to end his grief. His shortsighted self-pity beliefs were what validated his actions with the hope of joining them. The question for all viewers should be, "Why was he allowed to live without his family?" His loneliness became a stumbling block to what God had intended by keeping him alive. Sometimes when tragedy strikes, we blame God.

When there is no one to blame for some fatality, God becomes the culprit. These accusations are falsified when our relationship with the Lord is not as close as it should be. A rebellious heart will always seek excuses to remain in darkness. Only the Blood of Christ was given as the gift of atonement for sin. Therefore, Judas Iscariot who hung himself because of his choice to betray the Son of God could have sought forgiveness by repenting as did the thief on the cross.

Many people have given sacrificially for the furtherance of physical existence. Their contributions have served well the purposes intended, yet they themselves died in their sins and are separated from the Holy Just God forever. Now if you will follow me along the pages of Scripture for another example of "gift giving." Let us journey with Jesus and His disciples to observe an incident occurring at the home of a Pharisee. Approaching the door's entrance, we hear voices from some of the distinguished guests. Their purpose for congregating seems to be a customary habit. The owner, Simon, grabs this opportunity so he and his friends can get closer to Jesus and chat with Him.

This Jewish teacher already suspected this invitation was not only for a meal that day. The disciple, John Mark, pens this intriguing narration and includes a gift-giving ceremony for us. This was a surprise for many, since it was done spontaneously. It also created tension among some of the men in the company. The recipient of the gift soon addresses this uncomfortable atmosphere, which has all the making of an intriguing love story. Let us fine-tune our ear-waves to this frequency and absorb the reason why the Son of God took time out to make this house call.

It was perhaps another casual day in the city of Nain. The complacent bewildering crowds in the neighborhood were following Jesus. As always, He was leading the procession on that hot and dusty road to an up-scale town house in the village. I believe he did not accept this invitation just for the meal, or to escape the meddling crowd. Perhaps it was to rest in a cooler atmosphere and share the message of the Kingdom of Heaven behind closed doors.

In chapter 7:36 to 50 we have this epistle of Dr. Luke mentioning a few things worth considering. He makes mention of the hospitality, the humility, honesty and the temptation the heart struggles with on a daily basis. He also encourages the reader to the end of his episode, leading to the foothills of Golgotha. Another disciple and writer was Mathew the tax collector. He also had some interesting bits and pieces to add (Matt. 26:10-12).

Together, they painted an unforgettable scene on the canvas of our minds. Those who knew the "teacher" soon realized He didn't make this house call for any of those comforts. Matthew squeezed through the clustered room beneath the thatch roof to find himself with a front-seat view. Jesus and Simon, amidst the invited guests were seated and enjoying the "catch of the day." Gazing uncomfortably were some religious leaders with itching ears and peeled eyes. As they began conversing with the "Rabbi" from Galilee, a shuffling at the back of the room was heard.

About halfway through their deliberations, a spontaneous, unexpected reaction came again from the clustered room. The dimly lit room felt the warmth of the evening sunbeams nesting gently against the backdrop of the red clay walls. A familiar figure of graceful beauty began to approach them. Her commonly dressed apparel stirred curiosity and created an astounding few moments of silence. The eyes of the religious leaders were glued on her, as she meticulously headed towards the teacher.

Watching in amazement for the outcome of her actions, a soft whispering began in the shadowed corners of the room as she went and sat at Jesus' feet. Thoughts of indifference mixed with condemnation had already infiltrated the hearts of her customers who began stepping back into the unseen corners of the house. Others waited for a response from the owner of the house, as if it was time to throw her out. Not only was she not invited, but was considered by many to be a sinner marked by prostitution.

Therefore, Simon had all legitimate reason to have her thrown to the curious crowd in the yard. But when pride and prejudice can be shelved, even for the sake of curiosity, perhaps an event or miracle can happen when least expected. This became the element of surprise that even made the jaws of His disciples drop open in astonishment. And so it was, she came with tears of humility. In her hand, she held the most valuable of her acquired earthly possessions.

This precious gift would be given as a tribute of her devotion to the Rabbi. Her attitude demonstrated a pivotal point in God's redemption plan at hand. The journey to Golgotha had begun as Law (the law of man) and Grace (the grace of Almighty God) kissed each other goodbye. Matthew noticed how she reached upwards gently, loosened her hair and began wiping the feet of Jesus after pouring some of the perfumed ointment. The bulging eyes of resentment from the law keepers were astonished at her outrageous performance. Little did they realize she had already experienced the gift of faith?

Now she was demonstrating to her accusers the work of love received from the Son of God (1 Cor. 11:15). Her first lesson teaches us how to give with a genuine heart. It usually comes with an overwhelming spirit of compassion. Her displayed appreciation was an exemplary challenge to all followers of the Cross. Tiptoeing to unveil the practices in her culture that brought sarcasm and emotional discomfort, she smiled with contentment. Focusing with a heart of humility, this "spur of the moment" recognition will go down in history.

Her salvation was time-consuming work that transformed her heart. Although she had other options like a cooked meal, a bouquet of fresh flowers, or perhaps a new set of robes, she did not hesitate to be found in the house of a Pharisee. The religious leaders thought it was inappropriate, but those things never crossed her mind.

Her impulse was to sacrificially give the best she had without the hope of ever receiving any type of payment. If only for a short while, before being interrupted by the crowd, she could sit at His feet and glorify God. Not at the Master's request, but from a broken heart and with a contrived spirit, she began to worship the Son of God. Such an example of humility was never before witnessed by the "righteous folks" of that town. This genuine act resulted in her sanctification and justification with these words from the Master, "*Your faith has saved you, go in peace.*" Was it because of the type of gift or its worth that she received salvation? She sacrificially gave her treasured possession, a gift that was worth a year's wages according to Simon's son, Judas.

She laid it all at the Master's feet. Paul later appealed to followers of the Cross for a similar attitude in Romans 12:1. He beseeched every believer in Christ "*to present our bodies a living sacrifice.*" The Lord Jesus does not delight in offerings; He wants hearts that will surrender and willingly yield to His allegiance. Her desire would no longer be to dabble in the habit of prostitution. At that dramatic moment in time, all eyes focused as she poured the downy softness from the crown of His head to the soul of His feet. In return for her devotion, she received a greater gift than any man could have ever given her, more satisfying than the pleasures life had to offer. His gift in return was eternal life, which no man can purchase, or negotiate.

From His heart to hers, it was expressed through the joy of tears never before witnessed in that region of Galilee. No wonder the skeptics had questions, and so did some of His disciples. Nevertheless, from the fragrant oil came that diffusion of His knowledge to all hearts present. "*They keep hearing but did not understand, they keep on seeing, but did not perceive,*" as the prophet said in Isaiah 6:9. For my fourth example on the topic of gift giving, allow me to go deeper than our money purses. This one is heading into the pipelines of our bodies.

Our veins are the passage ways to the body. They carry a liquid designed and capable of sustaining life. This liquid is not compatible to any other liquids found in our system, nor is it possible to reproduce it with "ALL" it capabilities. When our Creator designed and formed us, this liquid was introduced to mobilize each tissue, limb and muscle. When it is isolated for medical purposes, various components can be extracted or introduced to enhance the complexity of its composition.

It has with today's technological advancement that flexibility; and at the same time is susceptible to contamination. To some degree it can be replaced, but man is not capable of inducing its life-giving proprieties. Only through the Creator who *"breathed into his nostrils, the breath of life, and man became a living soul"* (Gen. 2:7b).

Regardless of color, race, or creed within the entire human civilization, the blood system is universal for survival. It was that "breath of physical life" which was drained from the Son of God on a Roman cross for sinners like me. It became the only sacrifice God the Father accepted that would liberate a sinful race. Within designated areas of hospitals and health care facilities, signs like this are customarily seen: "**Give the gift for life.**" What is it the Almighty Creator did that has become the centrality of human existence in this unique liquid? Apart from His breath of life, no one is capable of permanently sustaining life regardless of how many blood transfusions.

Every created being carries a blood formula that is weaved into our DNA. Wrapped in the complexity is that mystery we call life. It comes with the capacity to allows expressions of our mind and emotional feelings (Lev. 17:11). Without His breath, humans would be cheap, expendable, and easily replaced. I am aware of the history of slavery and its current day practices around the world. The exploitation on human trafficking has filled the coffers of modern pirates. The struggle for supremacy over earthy wealth and power in the hands of dictators has passed down to today's generations. We have mastered the art of treating others with scant courtesy, even among those we referee to "brothers and sisters."

The Holy Bible makes mention of "blood" with its remarkable and intriguing history. It will fathom us into an eternity of our choosing. This bloody journey began on the sixth day of Creation for God's intents and purposes. Observe the imagery of the Creator as He dabbles His hands in clay (*"formed man of the dust of the ground"*). Then came the intriguing miracle of life, (*"and breathed into his nostrils the breath of life"*) Gen. 2:7.

Genesis 3:21 reveals how the Lord provided a covering for Adam and Eve. Under the circumstances, it was susceptible to the raging elements they were about to face. It had to take place with the shedding of blood. That hide, and not the leaves, were adequate for covering their shame and guilt. God made them tunics after sacrificing an animal.

Thereafter, a sacrificial act became atonement for their sins over a period of time. *"And according to the law almost all things are purified with blood, and without the shedding of blood there is no remission of sins"* (Heb. 9:22). Almost all things including animal blood were not totally sufficient for the remission of past, present, and future sins.

The next paragraph brings out the importance of the gift for life humanity received over two thousand years ago. No more sacrificing or searching for peculiar animals and birds to offer the God of all creation. No need for idol worship. No need for the sacrament of penance or deeds of self-mortification to have your sins forgiven.

A perfect gift for life was sent by God to be the total substitute for all our sins. As the shepherds witnessed the angels singing and the villagers rejoicing, the Messiah was born in fleshly apparels (Lk. 2:8-13). Thirty-three and a half years later, it came to pass as the crowds gathered with His chosen apostles to witness his ascension (1 Cor. 15:6). The prophet Samuel reminded the worshipers of Israel when he wrote, *"Hath the Lord as great delight in burnt offerings and sacrifices, as in obeying the voice of the Lord?"* (1 Sam. 15:22a).

Abraham, willing to sacrifice his son, was not entering into pagan worship. If he was, it would contradict Moses, the Lord's servant, with instructions regarding blood sacrifices and atonement for sins. The book of Leviticus, chapter 17:11 gives an educational view about "blood" and "sacrifices" performed before the death of Jesus Christ. The Bible says, *"For the life of the flesh is in the blood, and I have given it to you upon the altar to make atonement for your souls, for it is the blood that maketh atonement for the soul."*

Therefore, in favor of humanity, the Lord God took the initiative to provide a perfect sacrifice. This agreement in Genesis 3:15 became the first "human rights declaration" between God and Satan at the scene of the crime transpired in the Garden of Eden in Paradise. It was the first covenant made, *"Not with the blood of goats and calves, but with His own blood He entered the most holy place once for all"* (Heb. 9:12). His "sakra-fiss" as the Greeks referred to it as, was that gift of His life for our lives.

This is why the Apostle Paul refreshed the minds of believers with these words, *"We do not wrestle against flesh and blood, but against principalities, against powers, against the rulers of the darkness of this age, against spiritual hosts of wickedness in heavenly places"* (Eph. 6:12). Without the shedding of Christ's blood, there is no remission of sins for all people. It is why *"God so loved the world that He gave His only begotten Son, that whoever believes in Him should not perish but have everlasting life."* Even with the aid of modern medical therapy and herbal remedies, mankind cannot alleviate his guilty conscience. No religious or humanitarian "good deeds" are able to equate for a sinful heart. *"He was wounded for our transgressions, He was bruised for our iniquities, the chastisement of our peace was upon Him, and with his stripes we are healed"* (Isa. 53:5). Therefore, forgiveness comes only through Jesus Christ. My prayer will forever be to *"Examine me, O Lord, and prove me, try my reins and my heart"* (Ps. 26:2). But please remember, I'm dust, and life is fragile.

Job recognizes his limitations in chapter 14:1 & 2. He said, *"Man who is born of woman is of few days and full of trouble; he comes forth like a flower and fades away, he flees like a shadow and does not continue."* Every day God allows the "living" person 86,400 seconds of "free will" choices. With His free gift for life, comes this promise to me: *"He will never leave me nor forsake me as an orphan"* (Jn. 14:18).

Chapter Seven

THE BEST IS YET TO COME

In conclusion, I pen this final chapter by recapping from each of the previous chapters. To execute this justly, I will zoom in on specific areas that I hope will pull tightly into focus the book's topic "Consider Your Ways." It is my intention to weave a tapestry of hope for curious minds. However, I will remind my readers that each person is uniquely wired. Males and females have the God-given ability to choose what type of spiritual, physical, and mental strengths they want to possess and achieve. Each will determine if it is good, better, or in their best interest of worth to make sacrifices.

Regardless of what method you choose or which "deity" you worship; we all have choices. With these comments allow me to whole-heartedly encourage you to approach each segment with faith and reasoning. Both of these inner ingredients are beneficial for emotional stability. I pray some form of digestible mediation will be accomplished. Bear in mind that *"the heart is deceitful,"* so, *"be wise as a serpent,"* even if truth kills (Jer. 17:9; Matt. 10:16).

Remember, the mind should not decide if something is true until you've looked at the data. It is my belief that every human being who ever experiences life on Earth (past-present-future) will have a different story to relate before the Creator (1 Cor. 3:13). Since there are several schools of thoughts about the "spiritual" realms of the supernatural, we must use truth as the plumb line.

Over the centuries, man has drifted from his integrity and soiled his conscience with uncertain practices of accountability. Without the conscientiousness of God, he often finds difficulty in distinguishing right from wrong. When such is the case, he finds himself outside the boundaries of truth. In today's corporate society, some religions have shifted their moral values to accommodate the convenience of temporary pleasures. Children from these societies have difficulty in following instructions. As a young boy, I had to welcome discipline with tolerance, even when it was not desirable.

To align my thoughts with sound reasoning, I went to the Word of God. I had to depend on the Holy Spirit. As a result, I find comfort in my environment with appreciation for the code of moral ethics. Therefore, any society I am partaking in enables me to grow physically, spiritually, and mentally towards a comfortable lifestyle. My journey in life would have been more difficult without my caretakers. In return, I am now investing in what I have gained to "spend" my remaining years with those entrusted to me.

Sharing knowledge and education to strengthen tomorrow's generation is a goal on my daily calendar of life. To my atheist and agonistic friends, I beg this question: Have you ever looked at the evidence on whether God exists or not, before rejecting him? To the religionist: how do you determine which the "true" God to worship? On sleepless nights, my heart would experience a paralysis of fear pondering over careless choices my unsaved friends and family members are making in regards to their final destination.

This pain comes by investing in lives of people you love and care about. The un-churched folks seldom realize how uncertain life is. It is good that most Christians think about not spending eternity in that God-forsaken place the Bible refers to as Hell. So it is incumbent of me to ensure each of you about the free gift of salvation. During the course of our lives, I'm sure many, if not all of you, have at some given period experienced unpleasant circumstances. I assume most of those experiences came during the younger years of your lives.

Now in some mysterious ways those strange experiences gradually vanish when the early years of maturity begins. Then we quickly forget how life often throws things at us when least expected. I recall disappointments and trials blaming my parents or others when hasty conclusions arrive. Nevertheless, I am learning by God's grace to take responsibility for my actions. I am also learning to accept each day as a blessing instead of complaining. Let me encourage you to accept the outcome of your actions, even if they surprise you. Then in the process of time and by the will of God, I pray healing will come.

By nature, we are all imperfect, therefore mistakes will occur along life's journey. However, there is a small marginal difference with some who keep practicing their mistakes instead of learning from them. To avoid repetition, I find discernment when I consider the options God has placed before me. With each person, our predicaments will differ, so I'm not anxious to weary the listening ears of my caring friends. Nor should a troubled heart find gossiping lips to confide in. At times, I find myself overly anxious, jumping to inappropriate conclusions.

My first topic for review will be, "It came to pass." I am only to complete this book and fulfill one of the ambitions on my "to do list." Then it will have come to pass. However, there are many areas of my life which have come to pass by the grace and mercy of Almighty God. This book is not the final episode of things coming to pass. From the early beginning, my interest in Bible knowledge has taught me more about relating to my family, my friends, and myself.

Observing Bible literature I have gained from a variety of events things which have come to pass. No only beneficial to me, but educating in my journey of faith regarding the Sustainer of our Universe. My budding years came with opportunities of seeing, touching, smelling, and tasting fragments of His existence. Many unchurched likewise have also testified to a greater being than mortal man. Christians refers to Him as the Triune GOD.

My journey of knowledge also provided knowledgeable interest regarding some of the world's famous historians. Those who made enormous contributions to the welfare of the human race have paved the path for success today. Since time began, the preservation of history has enabled mankind to trace the validity of various civilizations. As a result, I now have access to a "family tree" to reflect my ancestors. By faith, I trust in the researcher's knowledge and those who made it possible for availability, even though I don't know them. Then I can compare notes and say such and such has come to pass.

Therefore, with all the historical events surrounding the person of Jesus Christ, why are so many choosing to ignore His credentials? Those who do not read or take an interest in biblical predictions have world events for consideration. Perhaps I believe it is easier to choose what will accommodate our sinful nature. If I have reason to deny by way of excuses, these will pacify my conscience. It is natural for man outside the realm of divine intervention to become questionable about the validity of researches done by biblical scholars. However, in the same breath, the general consensus is to accept the Roman Emperor Cesare Augustus. He will accept the great rulers of the ancient world, before the Jewish man from Galilee. Anyone who will not pose a threat or demand accountability from me will be easy to accept. As my eldest brother once said to me, *"There is none so blind as those who refuse to see."*

To comment on the second chapter's title "Which journey are you on?" I will review John 14:6. In His declaration to the disciple Thomas, Jesus emphasized human frailty and the lack of wisdom regarding the way to eternity. Prior to His imminent departure, He reassured them of His position in the God Head (Matt. 28:18) with these words, *"I am the way, the truth, and the life, no man cometh unto the Father, but by me"* (Jn. 14:6).

Unlike other religious leaders, Jesus said HE is the way, not a way. He is the truth, not some form of enlightenment. "This Man's Word became His Bond." He fulfilled prophecies that were foretold hundreds of years before His birth. Throughout Scripture we read of events coming to pass. The remaining prophecies recorded in the book of Revelation tell me that the best is yet to come. His Kingdom will come and those who are prepared know the best is yet to come. (Eph. 3:6). It is a place beyond man's wildest comprehension.

My soul will find perfect rest among citizens of Heaven. From the dawn of time man began entangling himself with inculcated habits and vague options. His quest for inner peace, genuine love, and total satisfaction outside the will of God is like a distant mirage. He displays a sense of hostility towards unfamiliar faces who disagree with him. I have observed in my short years how man has become a mobile race with temporal values. We often use the phrase "the sky is the limit" even though we are venturing beyond Earth's crust.

At the entrance of knowledge, my heart begins to pant towards a prosperous life. One I hoped would have had nothing to do with pain, stress, and disappointments. Then with the bliss of God's grace and salvation, my life took on a different perspective. I began to realize it is far better to obey God than search for worldly prosperity.

Man today continues to ask Jesus the same question Pontius Pilot asked: *"Do you have a kingdom?"* (Jn. 18:36).

God the Father said *"Behold, the tabernacle of God is with men, and He will dwell with them"* (Rev. 21:3). The Christian God is the God of Omniscience, Omnipresence and Omnipotence (Ps. 139:1-16). It is why He is capable of *"instructing us, teaching us, guiding us and to watch over us"* (with emphasis). Anyone who does not (yet) have Kingdom status should know He said, *"But the fearful, and unbelieving, and the abominable, and murderers, and whoremongers, and sorcerers, and idolaters and all liars, shall have their part in the lake"* (Ps. 32:8 with emphasis).

The lake refers to Hell; that place *"which burneth with fire and brimstone, which is the second death"* (Rev. 21:8 with emphasis). All the evidence relating to His advent birth, His preaching, and teaching ministry came to pass. When the appointed time came for His death, burial, and resurrection, history declared validation.

The day turned into night, the Earth trembled, and man witnessed impossible things coming to pass. The Bible tells us *"There is only one mediator between God and man."* Jesus Christ is that person qualified to take my prayer before Almighty God (Heb. 8:6; 12:24; 1 Tim. 2:5-6). The Bible is the Christian's G.P.S. (General Positional System) that supplies basic instruction before leaving Earth. It comes not from religious traditions, nor from man's philosophical knowledge.

It comes from *"God, who at various times and in various ways spoke in time past to the fathers by the prophets, has in these last days spoken to us by his Son"* (Heb. 1:1). His name shall be called Emanuel, Counselor and Prince of Peace. It was *"God also bearing witness both with signs and wonders with various miracles and gifts of the Holy Spirit according to His will"* (Heb. 2:4). *"As for God, His way is perfect; the word of the Lord is proven, He is a shield to all who trust in Him"* (Ps. 18:30).

So my unsaved friend, with all these promises and fulfillments in Scripture, do you believe the best is yet to come? The third chapter entitled "Growing up is optional" can be taken for granted by adults. Children who are treated with scant courtesy or face unpleasant circumstances often hide under this umbrella of fear. This parental proverb has a taste of perceptiveness for any family unit. King Solomon reached the heartbeat of his people with simplicity. He spent time listening, observing, and responding to them.

His method was through writing similes and catchy wisdom. These were used as common songs throughout the ancient world (1 Kin. 4:29-33). Today's eloquent minds have also found food for thought with his legacy of wisdom. Likewise, in the progress of modern education, clichés evolve like *"the hand that rocks the cradle, rules the world."* Though it is not biblically related, it carries some implications worth considering. Those who look after the babies will have the time to impart some form of knowledge. This input will eventually become a foundational block for that child to stand upon. Parents sometime do not consider the influential impact that comes with neutering young life.

It is rumored that humans learn three quarters of all their education between the ages of one to seven years. This means habits, moral values, and wise choices that will shape the future of that child are imperative to *"train up a child in the way he /she should go."* (Prov. 22:6 with emphasis) that is God's way. Parents are temporary guardians who are admonished to *"not withhold good from those to whom it is due, when it is in the power of your hand to do so"* (Prov. 3:27). If only more adults were mindful of what they say and do; children are "little people" with sharp minds. We can avoid them from having to reap the pains and sorrow we caused as parents.

I am grateful for my parents and siblings in attending to my needs over the fleeting years. The Bible tells the story of a woman of substance. Her name was Hannah, and she had an urgent prayer request. After much prayer and supplication her prayer was answered. In return she made a commitment to the Lord. Her son, Samuel, would be given over to the temple priest for training. This would be for his remaining life (1 Sam. 1:10-12).

Children can be very good imitators who have sharp minds and clear ears behind closed doors. Adult church members sometimes forget their responsibility to all children with who they have made voids with during a baptism service. They are to gently and tactfully implement the respect and courtesy often disregarded at home and school. King Solomon speaking to his son in Proverbs 10:9 said *"The man of integrity walks securely, but he who takes crooked paths will be found out."* I live in a society where some parents depend on the television for their child's early education. Without censorship they allow full viewing to children who are yet to learn about desecration all in the name of some peace to be alone.

Those who live by shortcuts may eventually be disappointed. While shortcuts can bring rewards depending on circumstances, it will not work when it comes to worshipping God. It was never God's intension for humans to live in ways that rob them of His blessings. His purpose to prosper us has one condition. My mother's book of clichés says, "*You can't bend an old tree.*" From my childish thoughts I'd whisper, "*Why try to bend it, when you can just cut it down?*" So you see, "*foolishness is also bound up in the heart of children*" (Prov. 22:15). As a child my concept on the truth differentiated into two categories.

Depending on the severity of the matter and on which side of the fence you live, handling the truth often involved some careless assumptions. Fabricating can become a daily practice if there is no fear for God. A dear friend and pastor once said to his congregation: "*An excuse is the skin of a reason stuffed with a lie*" (Reverend David Beckmann). The Lord God said we should "*Lie not one to another*" (Col. 3:9). In the cycle of life, "*Children are a reward from the Lord*" (Ps. 127:3). Adults often forget they are "gifts" not "possessions" to display as ornaments.

When our daughter, Melissa, became part of our lives, circumstances had to change so we could share our blessing with her. She eventually became our representative wherever she went. I would remind her that a good name is better than riches; it is your passport to life in any country.

We had to always display a lifestyle that she could use as a stepping stone in growing her own family. I realize that it has been the best investment we have made. Today by God's grace her contribution of three grandchildren allows my wife and me to continue investing in their lives so God will eventually get the Glory.

The legacy of faith in them is to perpetuate other lives Christ died for and stand against the disobedience and transgression of ignorant minds that walk in darkness. A surrendered life will learn of the perceptiveness to victory, and have his eyes opened to things never before seen. Growing older in God's grace is a privilege and not a coincident. In the fourth chapter entitled "Know Jesus or No Jesus," there are issues of interest that adds to the deliberations. I will use 2 Timothy 3:16 as stepping stones to summarize my objectives.

Very distantly we have the three basic elements for spiritual growth contextually preserved through the annals of time. Even today this helps me cultivate faith to benefit from failures, reproof, and correction. I am not fond of bitter medication, yet it has done me good in times of need. Like following explicit instructions to avoid repeating mistakes, my conscience guards me from ungodly practices. With obedience, I always gain productivity relying on God's word.

"All scripture is given by inspiration of God, and is profitable for doctrine, for reproof, for correction, for instruction in righteousness; that the man of God may be perfect, thoroughly furnished unto all good works." I am thankful to the many saints who have encouraged me. They have supported me in prayer and at times walked along side my journey with me. Like our Lord Jesus, brothers and sisters are to be thoroughly furnished unto all good works and not to misguide others with flattering words of deceit (Jn. 3:16).

In my fifty plus years of journeying with the Lord, I have found Him to be reliable and trustworthy. He is the Author of my faith, and is always present in times of chaos and human disappointments. In His words I find comfort and joy among other blessings on a regular basis. I am not searching for another savior because He did not allow His persecution, His shame, His reproach and His death to stop Him from attending to my cares. One of the inspired writers known as Apostle Paul admonished a young believer and close friend named Timothy. He told him to *"hold fast the form of sound words* (doctrine).*"*

As it was in the beginning, even so today people from all walks of life are searching for satisfaction or contentment. Many willingly offer financial and material donations with the hope of a just reward to gain inner peace. The peace many seek is not to be confused with temporal gestures of pleasures acquired. Those methods don't have the hope and love Christ offers (2 Tim. 1:13). Paul reminds young Timothy in 2 Timothy 3:14 -15 that, *"He must continue in the things which you have learned and been assured of, knowing from whom you have learned them; and that from a childhood* (around 5 years) *you have known the Holy Scriptures."* This means we should not become "pew jumpers" for the sake of unconfessed sins. It was during His ministerial years with the disciples the Lord Jesus addressed skepticism. Whenever it surfaced among the meddling crowds, His rhetorical answers silenced even the Scribes and Pharisees who were regularly seeking ways to criticize His teaching. During such an occasion, Matthew recorded how they exalted *"traditions above the divine law"* (Matt. 15:1-20). This story lends itself to where the disciples were accused of eating without washing their hands. Jesus takes up this accusation and reproves them about their ceremonialism.

Even today there are religious folks who don't want *"instruction in righteousness"* or to be reminded that *"we all have sinned"* (Rom. 3:23). Only the Son of God was able to capture the true essence of righteousness when He said, *"For I say unto you, that except your righteousness shall exceed the righteousness of the Scribes and Pharisees, ye shall in no case enter into the kingdom of heaven"* (Matt. 5:20). They were seeking to establish their own righteousness (through the law) so they would not have to submit to God's righteousness (Rom. 10:3).

This is still common among our decent moral citizens and religious worshipers whose pride, arrogance, and perverse mouth the Lord hates (Prov. 8:13). In most civil courts, the judicial system declares that a person is innocent until proven guilty. God's judicial system says, *"There is none righteous, no not one"* (Rom. 3:10). A cultural Christian lives by the majority rule of his mind which amounts to the "average churchgoers." Those who use religion like a cloak of hypocrisy have failed to realize Christianity is not an idea.

Neither is it a philosophical system like Buddhism or a code of morals ethics like Islam. Common ritual practices can overwhelm one's feelings of modesty. They can also misguide the pure value of the Cross during a worship service. Christianity should become a true-life drama. Every moment is worth experiencing with the Savior. Pastor Mark Denver had this to say in his book, "What is a Healthy Church?" He explained how *"a Christian is someone who has reached the end of himself, and his own moral resources"* (First Baptist Church of Capitol Hill, Washington D.C.).

When I consider the ancient believers who were seekers of *"the way,"* my zeal to know more challenges me to dig deeper in the Word for strength to help in times of need. Although many early believers were persecuted, it did not prevent or dull their enthusiasm. Our modern civil right movements have brought much freedom for religions. It has also open doors to other cults which are doing greater harm to societies infested with "cultural" practices.

Those who have suffered oppression due to the Christian faith will know the answer to this question. However, for many who are yet to experience some form of resentment, here is something to ponder upon. *"If you were taken to court charged for being a Christian, would there be sufficient evidence to convict you?"* Hardly would a "good man" in today's society want to be interrupted from his personal peace for the cause of Jesus Christ. These types of interruptions could have some drastic repercussions, especially for those who are making their living by what they get.

That is contrary to the born-again who makes his life by what he gives according to Matthew 5:42. Peter was asked by Jesus, *"Who do you say that I am?"* Later on in the conversation Jesus said to his disciples, *"For whoever is ashamed of Me and My words in this adulterous and sinful generation, of him the Son of Man also will be ashamed when He comes in the glory of His Father with the Holy Angels"* (Mk. 8:29- 38). In the following years after Jesus left the Earth, the Apostle Paul had this to say from prison in Rome, *"For I am not ashamed of the gospel of Christ"* (Rom. 1:16a). He continued writing with these words, *"For me to live is Christ and to die is gain"* (Phil. 1:20).

After his transformation from fisherman to preacher, Peter endured persecution even while he was encouraging other followers of the Cross. In one of his epistles he said to them, *"If you are reproached for the name of Christ blessed are you; if anyone suffers as a Christian, let him not be ashamed"* (1 Pet. 4:14a & 16a). Those simple fishermen gave up their permanent jobs and went beyond the extremes at the cost of their lives. They wanted to know more about this Savior; saying no would have entailed the loss of the best that was yet to come.

For consideration on the fifth chapter, "Christians among other believers" I will focus on what Matthew the disciple heard and wrote from Jesus regarding the "Wheat and the Tares (tears)." Like all parables about the Kingdom of Heaven, this one has a twist. Jesus said to *"let both grow together until the harvest."* Let us consider who or what are the "wheat" and the "tears." Knowing what these represent would help us to understand why the Son of God made such a statement. The wheat is considered to be those who heard and obey the word of God. The tears are those who refuse and rebel against the teaching of Jesus Christ.

In this analogy, both seeds are allowed to grow together until the time of the harvest. *"At the time of harvest I will say to the reapers, first gather together the tares."* Again Jesus makes a striking remark by instructing the tears to be gathered first. Should it not be that the wheat is more valuable to gather first? Sometimes the Christian thinks that the unbelieving community around him is getting first preference and seems to be prospering more or better than him.

It can be frustrating to see evil folks around you enjoying similar things that you had to sweat and sacrifice to accomplish. But wait for the final remarks from the Lord regarding the harvest. He says to *"bind them* (the tears) *in bundles to burn them."* No recycling, because they have no value. However, *"the wheat will be gathered and put into His barn."* Contrary to eastern culture, the Western gardeners in the Caribbean basin often get rid of the weeds regularly before harvesting.

Those who refused to accept Him will eventually be destroyed. These are the counterfeit followers who become very religious by sacrificing their time, talents, and finances to a church agenda. They don't need a Savior or Lord to tell them how to live. The second instruction is to gather the valuables. This represents the born again believers that comprise the universal church. The barn is Heaven, and you can work the math for where the tears go.

When Jesus said to all who will follow Him *"take up your cross and follow after me"* (Matt. 10:38). He was speaking to people who are willing to give up their daily routine in life, to become uncomfortable for His sake. These are followers willing to leave behind worldly "things and stuff" to do His will. Worldly things can become more valuable than a lost soul living next door. Some things have a high cost of maintenance that can demand most of our time. (In essence, no strings attached to those going on field missions.)

Today's "freedom fighters" implore force and strenuous rules to obey before obtaining acceptance into their elite sect. These leaders bask in the glory of comfort and convenience, while their followers pay the price with tears, sweat, and blood. I wish more Christians had an answer for this bumper sticker sign: *"What on earth are you doing for*

Heaven's sake? Jesus preached, taught, and healed in the affirmation of the Kingdom of Heaven (Matt. 3:1).

It is why his disciples did not remain silent behind closed doors after his death. The kingdom of Heaven and God are not fables as some religious groups propagate. Had there been no resurrection, then Christians would not have any hope of the best to come.

Although I have life, a will to choose and the education to survive, my success depends on what Christ said in 2 Corinthians 12:9. *"My Grace is sufficient for you; my strength is made perfect in weakness,"* Dr. D. James Kennedy penned in his book, *"Doctrine Then Duty, Precept and Then Practice."* (Delighting God). As an elder in my home church, I knew how easily duty and practice sometimes takes priority on my busy schedule. Depending on self-reliance and experience to get the job done is normal, outside the will of God.

I often forget that Christians are not perfect people, but just Saints of God. These are the comments of Pastor Thabiti Anyabwile, *"When I consider the word "Christian" in this context, I'm seeking among followers of the faith, those who possess a character that is increasingly reflecting God's character revealed in His word."* The unsaved person considers himself to be perfect without the need for divine forgiveness. They emulate a worldly character.

My native land displays many religious denominations, some carrying the name brand of eastern cultures. Integrated in their practices is pride. It fosters the mother of invention to the "chosen frozen" at Boredom Hill Chapel. My Christian journey allows me the privilege of seeing where Christ came to "shake" and not "shape" history (Matt. 10:34 & 35). His plan for History is always on track with a purpose. While the world sinks with its rebels, leaders are conforming to unbiblical practices.

Every new day I'm given the privilege to consider what the Lord Jesus said to His disciples at the Passover meal. He said *"This do in remembrance of Me."* In this context, He is introducing the communion table. Then before leaving for Heaven said to them, *"Teach them* (new converts) *to observe all things that I have commanded you"* (Matt. 28:20 & Lk. 22:19). If I am not obeying Him here on Earth, why do I want to live with Him in Heaven? Therefore, imposters who shade under the umbrella of Christianity need to decide who they will serve.

Popularity and favoritism, like two peas in a pod, obtain their nutrients from worldly standards and do not conform to biblical teaching (Matt. 7:15). The Apostle Peter in writing to the early church saints said, *"But there were also false prophets among the people"* (in the Old Testament times) *"even as there will be false teachers among you"* (today - New Testament times) *"who will secretly bring in destructive heresies, even denying the Lord who bought them"* (2 Pet. 2:1a). The world, the flesh, and the devil are distractions that will prevent anyone from seeking or serving the Risen Christ.

It encourages weariness and loses appetite for camping out in the Word. Neglecting the fellowshipping with the saints also widens the gap of separation. Jesus said, *"And ye shall know the truth, and the truth shall make you free"* (Jn. 8:32). Deceptiveness and craftiness should be examined with the help of God's word. Jesus said, *"For the tree is known by his fruit"* (Matt. 12:33b). In spite of the corrupt society Jesus was born into, He demonstrated practical holiness. He did it for them and us so we can emulate Him at work, school, home, and play.

Now I will move on to the sixth chapter which is titled, "Give the gift for life." I will focus on the phase *"Present your bodies a living sacrifice"* (Rom. 12:1b). This is an admonition with an obligation from the Apostle. Although during that period, followers were hunted down and persecuted or killed, here Paul reminded them of the cost to take up their cross and follow the Risen Christ. Followers of Jesus soon realized that their lives would be in jeopardy. Yet they continued sacrificially to spread the gospel with joy. If this "gift for life" were addressed to only the physical anatomy, then only those who mindfully desire pain and suffering would obtain it. I believe all challenges pertaining to sacrifices usually affect some form of mental, physical, and spiritual sphere of our being.

Just like the fluid agent that transcends throughout my entire being which keeps every segment functioning, similarly His breath of life goes through the smallest veins of my body.

This was as mind-blowing to the Psalmist as it is to the brilliancy of medical minds today. It is what brings that compelling desire Christians have every morning to give thanks for life. When the Son of God cried out, *"It is finished"* (Jn. 19:30) as He hung on that Roman Cross, it meant God's redemption plan of salvation for all of humanity had been completed to perfection. There is no need for humans to do sacrilegious offerings or bodily harm to themselves. That promise made in the Garden of Eden among Adam, Eve, and Satan came to pass.

The angels made a proclamation as the Son of God entered the Earth's atmosphere that first Christmas (Gen. 3:15). I often question my worth during prayer times, as did the Psalmist: "*What is man that He* (Almighty God) *should be mindful of* me?" (Ps. 8:4 with emphasis). In spite of man's hostility towards Jesus Christ, His mercy will continue to be extended for all sinners until He returns. The demonic scheme to devalue the soul was orchestrated with thirty pieces of silver. It may not be important where you come from, but it is to where you are going.

The longest journey sometimes can be from the head to the heart. Our global conditions make it difficult to believe "*the best is yet to come.*" Many are being persecuted and perishing for the cause of personal ideologies. Regardless of where you are stationed in life, every country in this world has its challenges. Both saved and unsaved often face the same circumstances. However, making choices are different and can be difficult, if you do not have Jesus Christ as your Counselor. Nevertheless, He continues to send rain and sun upon the just and the unjust (Matt. 5:45).

Every day we are seeing, hearing, watching, and reading about biblical revelations coming to pass. Christians may not agree with the ungodly political world leaders who are juggling for supremacy, but the Lord is using them to fulfill his purposes. There are many without the hope of the best that is yet to come. Some are seeking answers to the fear and uncertainty surrounding their homes and families. Those who prefer to remain neutral are contemplating religion and world views to put their faith to rest. The Apostle James said these folks are "*double minded persons who are unstable in all their ways*" (James 1:8 with emphasis).

The former Youth for Christ President, Dr. Torrey E. Johnson, commented at a youth rally in 1945, that his faith and hope in what he envisioned for the future of the ministry was global integration. He said to the gathered crowd, "*The best is yet to come.*" Decades later, in 2008, my wife and I attended a global Youth for Christ gathering in Gauteng South Africa. During the seven days of fellowship with over eighty-five nationalities in attendance, we witnessed the Lord blessing the nations in fulfilling Dr. Torrey's vision. The "**Come Ye Away and Rest Awhile**" (CYARA) training center in Magaliesburg was a melting pot where young and old committed to continue the preaching of the Gospel.

We believe the best is yet to come because Jesus said *"I go to prepare a place for you, and He's coming again to receive us; there we will be with him forever"* (Jn. 14:2-3 with emphasis). Heaven is a prepared place for a prepared people, are you getting ready? Jeremiah the prophet recorded these words of hope: *"For I know the thoughts that I think towards you, says the Lord, thoughts of peace and not of evil, to give you a future and a hope"* (Jer. 29:11). There have always been decent and upright citizens in the world. Many of them get involved with sacrificial commitments in the name of charity and goodwill gestures. Others go after dreams, hoping their sacrifices will eventually pay off in a hefty retirement plan. This is good and fitting in the eyes of man.

However, we have to be mindful that the rainbows we are chasing do not become our gods. While the Lord will honor our biddings, it is for us to also honor Him with worship and adoration with His body of believers. Those who toil will not go hungry, but be careful not to be anxious about storing up for moth and rust (Matt. 6:19). Some of the demands life throws at us like mortgage payments, insurance, and other living expenses can make us lose our focus as Christians. But those should be the least of concerns because if *"anyone is not found written in the Book of Life, they will be cast into the lake of fire"* (Rev. 20:15 with emphasis).

Several years after Jesus' farewell speech in Bethany, the apostle Paul began writing to the saints at Corinth. He said Jesus was seen by Cephas and the twelve apostles. He was also seen by over five hundred brethren at His resurrection (1 Cor. 15:5-6 & Lk. 24:50-51.). These people who witnessed His bodily ascension also knew the best was yet to come. Christians believe that *"the Lord Himself will descend from Heaven with a shout, with the voice of the archangel, and with the trumpet of God."*

There is no other religious deity who has made such a promise. There is no spiritual leader since time began to make such a claim.

When Christ returns, *"the dead in Christ will rise first. Then we who are alive and remain shall be caught up together with them in the clouds to meet the Lord in the air"* (1 Thess. 4:16-17). Another remarkable indication of His return was left in the stone grave recorded in John 20:1-10. To better understand the significance of what they saw, we have to journey back in time and observe their traditions.

Like most ancient divinations, the Near Eastern bible land civilization had their particular practice for burial. However, given the circumstances surrounding the beaten, crucified body of Christ, time was of the essence due to the commencement of the Sabbath Day. Therefore, those handling the proceedings did only the basic essentials before placing the body and sealing off the grave entrance. John the apostle said in his writing that it was Mary Magdalene who arrived first at the tomb.

When she saw the huge stone rolled away, her heart began pounding for fear of someone stealing the body. She nervously raced back to inform the sleeping disciples. Peter was among them and stirred drastic action, causing a race to the garden early that morning. They hurried to the site with puzzling thoughts of confusion. Winded with looks of skepticism, Simon Peter entered only to see *"the linen cloth Jesus was wrapped in"* on the slab of stone.

As the remaining disciples entered, a moment of silence struck all with only the echoes of Jesus' words resonating: *"Destroy this temple and in three days I will raise it up"* (Jn. 2:19). They also saw *"the handkerchief that had been around his head, not lying with the linen cloth but folded together in a place by itself."* Curious minds who are not familiar with burial customs of such times may ask: Why is there so much emphasis placed on describing the "handkerchief?" Why it was neatly folded and placed aside from the burial clothes?

What significance is this in regards to their culture? This explanation is another reason why Christian's believe the best is yet to come. Whenever the table was set for the master of his house by servants, everything that was placed on the table had to be furnished perfectly before the master was seated. The servant remained out of sight waiting for his master to complete dining. During which time the servant is constantly peeking for the signal from his master. This would be whether to clear the table or not. If the master momentarily leaves the table with the intension of returning, the servant dare not go near the table.

However, when he was finished and rose from the table, he'd wipe his hands and mouth and clean his beard. Then he wadded up the "napkin / handkerchief" and tossed it onto the table. That wadded napkin meant, "I'm done," so the table should be cleaned by the servant who was in waiting. However, if the master got up from the table and neatly *"folded his napkin,"* then laid it besides his plate and walked away, that servant dared not go near or touch the table. The folding of that napkin meant his master was coming back; he was not finished.

My unsaved friends, Jesus Christ the Son of God, the resurrected Lord of All Creation took the time to neatly fold and place the napkin separately from the linen cloth. It was to remind us of its significance that morning of the resurrection. He's coming back! Even in the valley of the shadow of death He continues to remind us that the best is yet to come. Perhaps you have reached a stage in your life where you feel useless. Life has become one big disappointment. There is no desire to even wake up in the morning. You feel worthless that life is fleeting by with regrets.

The Lord says do not fear, He will take you there. A place where all tears will be wiped away. Don't bring your treasures or try to defend what matters. He knows the darkest heart, be it grief or pain you bear, take it to Him in prayer. There is hope in Christ for all who are battered, even the lame, deaf, and weary. Death is swallowed up with victory, because His stripes have set captives free. Don't let tomorrow's fear rob you of today's joy. Don't be content to go on living a life of sublime.

You don't have to depart with just *"footprints on the sands of time"* (Henry Wadsworth Longfellow). Instead, leave a godly inheritance on the hearts along life's journey. Good memories of God's grace will always perpetuate a soul. Through faith you can say, the best is yet to come. *"For God has not given us the spirit of fear, but of power, and of love, and of a sound mind"* (2 Tim. 1:7). God's grace and mercy helps us shelve our concerns in the basement of our minds.

This is Dr. Steve Brady's suggestion: *"You don't need a full comprehensive knowledge of Jesus Christ before going to Him as your Savior"*

(Principal of Moorlands Bible College in England). This is how one apostle benefitted by following Jesus Christ: *"You were taught, with regard to your former way of life, to put off your old self, which is being corrupted by its deceitful desires; to be made new in the attitude of your minds; and to put on the new self, created to be like God in true righteousness and holiness"* (Eph. 4:22-23).

Remember my friend, ideas do have consequences. Learn to understand and evaluate them. Allow Christ to invade your life and fill you with contentment. You have been created to achieve something. My deceased friend, Pastor Tom Cook, once said to me: *"Confidence begets enthusiasm and enthusiasm conquers the world."* Don't believe feelings, experience, and thoughts are sufficient to rightly know God. We need more than forgiveness to enter Heaven.

THE ENGAGEMENT
RULES OF CHRIST

The Lord Jesus used a metaphor speaking about Himself as "the Bridegroom" and the universal church as "His Bride." He gave the Church instructions to observe before He returns again (Matt. 9:15.). A common phase I heard repeated as a young believer was *"Jesus is the answer."* However, not many Christians want to stop and listen to your questions. Everybody has a plan for my life, even when theirs is on the wrong track. When God found out about the problem "man" got himself into, He immediately provided the solution that would eradicate the virus referred to as sin (Gen. 3:1-24).

From then on *"it is appointed for men to die once"* (Heb. 9:27).

1. Because all have sinned. Rom. 3:22-26; Eph. 2:1-2.
2. Each person must confess. Rom. 10:10.
3. Believe in the finished work of Jesus Christ. 1 Tim. 2:5-6.
4. Accept Him by faith. Eph. 2:8; Rom. 10:8-13.
5. Be thankful for His gift of salvation. Rom. 10.

Prayer is to the Christian as water is to a fish; without a regular flow to either, life can become pretty dried up.

A Chinese proverb, *"When someone shares something of value with you, and you benefit from it, you have a moral obligation to share it with others."*

ABOUT THE AUTHOR

The author is a born and bred West Indian from the twin Republic Island of Trinidad and Tobago. He is the seventh of nine children from the loins of the late Mohammed and Rose Charles. His upbringing in the district of Siparia was an exciting and challenging experience. At the early age of eleven he received the gift of salvation with enthusiasm to grow in the council of God. During the fleeting years thereafter, his faithfulness and allegiance to the proclamation of the Gospel's message became the centrality of his existence. He is a foundational member from the inception of the Siparia Evangelical Church. He began serving the body of Lord as an usher.

As he attained greater wisdom and understanding, he began teaching in the Sunday school. His next step of obedience was the call to lead the weekly youth group. As a young, dedicated believer, he was also elected to serve as the Island's Director of the Evangelical Church's Youth Executive Board. His appetite for spiritual growth was rewarded when he was chosen to be one of three elders during low ebb at his home church's history. After thirty-eight years of fellowship among family, friends, and church members on the island, he with his beloved wife, Gloria, and precious daughter, Melissa, migrated to the Cayman Islands. Today he is permanently residing in Grand Cayman with his wife of forty-two years of blissful marriage.

His focus is on growing three grandchildren and keeping the bridge of support for Melissa and her husband, Ian, open as long as the Lord permits. Hamid and Gloria transferred their Trinidad membership in 1989 to be with the saints at Boatswain Bay Presbyterian Church. After ten years of involvement with the youth group, teaching adult Sunday school and being on the board of Elders, they made another transition. After a season of little congregational growth, they decided to relocate to the First Baptist Church of Grand Cayman in 1999. Not long after, he took up the challenge to continue teaching one of the adult Sunday school classes. Gradually he became involved with adult Sunday school class. He was also selected to take a term of office for three years as Director for Cayman Island Youth for Christ. One of many opportunities as the director was for he and his wife to attend the Youth for Christ International Conference in Magaliesberg, South Africa. His gift for teaching has overflowed into evangelism in mission work to Cuba and South Africa. He is currently serving the body of F.B.C. as one of many ushers and attending to his homegrown family. With fifty plus years of journeying with the Lord under his faith belt, he has completed his first book. His prayer is for all who read it to be become more obedient to their Creator by considering their ways.

Hamid Charles.

REFERENCE

Acknowledgement:

Lines from a hymn selected by Mrs. Penner currently residing in Portland, Oregon.

Introduction:

Proverbs 3:5-6 with emphasis; 22:6. 1 John 4:4 with emphasis. Jeremiah 29:11. Haggai 1:5-7. Matthew 7:13-30. John 14:6. Romans 12:1b. Philippians 3:14 with emphasis. 2 Timothy 3:16. Hebrews 12:1.

Chapter 1

Genesis 2:23; Job 19:26b; 7:17-18; 21:22; Psalm 51:5; 120:1; 142:2a; 7:11; 103:12; 127:3; 90:12 amplified. Proverbs 10:13; 5:1-2 with emphasis; 16:7; 3:5; 9:6; 1:19. Isaiah 55:11. Jeremiah 1:5. Ezekiel 22:30; Zechariah 2:8. Matthew 7:13; 18:2-5; 28:18-20; 19:16-22; Luke 16:13; 8:26-30; John 8:36; 3:16; 10:10b; 16:33b; Romans 15:4; 1 Corinthians 10:24. 2 Corinthians 5:7; Ephesians 2:19-20; 2:5-6 & 9; Philippians 3:7-8; 3:13b. Hebrews 12:2a; 11:25b; Colossians 3:20; 2 Peter 3:10; 1Timothy 3:16; Titus 3:5-6; 2 Peter 3:10; 7:17-18; 21:22. James 5:16; Revelations 16:16;

Jesus Among Other Gods, by Dr. Ravi Zacharias.

The Terminology for Liming, by H. Charles.

Queen Elizabeth 11. Christmas Message from The Caymanian Compass 28/12/84

Village of Siparia, excerpt from TriniViews.com

Chapter 2

Genesis 3:5 & 9; Exodus 16:1-36; Deuteronomy 32:35a. Psalm 91; 49:16-19; 1:10; 95:6-7; 24:3-5; 119:19; 1:1a; 32:8; 1:2; 119:9; 89:11; 33:5b-7; 89:11;

8:3a-4a; 37:25; 8:4a; 4:46; 127:3a. Proverbs 3:25-26; 16:18; 10:17; 1:7; 4:23; 21:2a; 12:15; 14:15; 15:13; 3:5-6; 30:7-8. Ecclesiastes 12:12b. Isaiah 55:8; 53:1-12; 40:6-8; Jeremiah 17:9. Micah 6:8. Matthew 13:3-8; 4:4 & 17; 8:1-6; 28:16-20; 11:28-29; Mark 16:19. Luke 22:42b; 4:33-35; 12:22-32; 13:29-30; 15:13-17; 5:40-42; 24:50-51; 24:6. John 14:1-6; 12:24; 3:19; 1:4; 16:33; 1:1; 20:17; 3:19; 8:44; 11:25; 8:36. Acts 9:3-5. Romans 3:23; 8:1 & 15 with emphasis; 3:23; 10:14; 1 Corinthians 4:14; 3:19; 1:18; 2:14. 2 Corinthians 12:7-9; 1:4; 9:8; 10:5; 1:18; 5:10. Ephesians 2:1-3; 1:7; Philippians 2:9-11 with emphasis; 4:6; 2:12b; 3:13b; 2:5. Colossians 3:17-21; 2:23. 1 Timothy 4:4 with emphasis. 5:13 & 17. 2 Timothy 4:4. 2 Thessalonians 3:11. Hebrews 13:5b; 9:27; 3:12; 10:25 & 31; 12:2a; 13:5b. James 1:8; 5:11. 1 John 1:1 & 8; 1 Peter 1:24; Revelations 20:14; 22:12b-19 with emphasis.

Chapter 3

Genesis 3:16-19; 2:7; 4:1. Jeremiah 17:9; 45:1-5; 6:16. Ezekiel 18:2; 11:12b. Psalm 101:2; 122: 1; 100:2 & 4; 23:1-6. Proverbs 10:12 with emphasis; 22:15a; 16:1; 1:5 & 22a; 13:20. Ecclesiastes 7:12 & 29; 9:10; 3:1 NIV; 12:8. Matthew 9:9; 26:34; 26:41; 10:38; Mark 16:19. Luke 2:52; 24:21. John 14:1-4; 15:4; 1:17; Romans 14:11; 8:5-8; 8:17 & 28; 3:3:10-12. 1 Corinthians 2:2. Ephesians 4:17b & 26; 2:11; 5:6 & 8; 6:1-4; 4:14. Philippians 2 :5; 3:9-14. Colossians 3:2; 1:27b. Hebrews 4:16.

Chapter 4

Genesis 3:3-29. Isaiah 55:6. Danial 3:16-18. Judges 16:28 & 29. Psalm 111:10; 23:3b; 29:11. Matthew 13:57 & 18-22, 16:18b; 13:1-9; 20:26; 1:18 & 20; 18:18. Luke 24:50-51. John 20:29; 17:3; 10 :15-30; 14:1-7 . Acts 4:12. Romans 15:4; 8:14; 1:25. 1 John 2:17 NIV. 1 Peter 1:4. 1 Corinthians 12:4-11. 2 Corinthians 12:16; 5:7. Ephesians 2:3 with emphasis; 5:6-7. Colossians 3:16 with emphasis. 2 Timothy 3:16. Hebrews 10:23; 11:1 & 6. Revelations 22:18-19.

Chapter 5

Genesis 6:1-3; 3:15; 2:7; 1 Samuel 15:22. Psalm 1:5; 116:15; 37:25; 51:1-11;147:11; 7:11. Proverbs 17:4; 15:11 & 22; 19:20; 14:12; 12:15; 1:5 & 8; 8:1; 3:5-6; 17:4; 15:11; Ecclesiastes 3:1-8 NIV; 12:14. Isaiah 26:3; 55:7-8 & 11; 53:4-5; 1:18; Matthew 7:20 & 25; 13:24-30; 26:41b; 26:36-47;

27:3-8; 7:15-19; 11:28-30; 50:20; 16:26b; 28:18-19; 8:28-32. Mark 1:21-24; Luke 11:38; 23:40-43; 24:13-30; 12:15; John 8:12 & 32;11:32; 14:2; 1:8; Acts 2:1-21. Romans 8:29; 12:3 & 6; 5:6 & 20b-21; 3:9 & 23;16:17-18; 1 Corinthians 15:56. Ephesians 2:1;6:12a; 6:11 & 17-18; Philippians 1:6. 1 Timothy 6:3; 4:2; 2; 2 Timothy 4:2; 1:7; 2:2-4. 2 Thessalonians 2:2-4. Hebrews 3:7-8; 11:16; 10:4 & 7-8 & 15. James 1:27; 4:1; 2:29. 1 Peter 5:8. 1 John 5:4b; 1:8-10; Revelations 20:10b; 22:12-13.

The Cross Centered Life, by C.J. Mahaney

World Religions, by Dr. Ravi Zachariah (Surah 17:15:35, 18. Ali & Hingorani 23).

Chapter 6

Genesis 3:21; 2:7b. Leviticus 17:11. 1 Samuel 15:22a. Job 41:1-2. Psalm 26:2. Isaiah 53:5; 6:9. Matthew 26:10-12. Luke 2:8-13. John 3:16; 14:1-2 7:18. Romans 12:1. 1 Corinthians 11:15; 15:6. Ephesians 6:12. Hebrews 9:12 & 22.

Chapter 7

Genesis 3:15. 1 Samuel 1:110-112. 1 Kings 4:29-33. Psalm 139:1-16; 133:1-16; 32:8; 18:30; 127:3; 8:4 with emphasis. Proverbs 3:27; 10:9; 22:15; 22:6. Jeremiah 17:9; 29:11. Matthew 10:16 & 34-35; 15:1-20; 5:42 & 45; 28:18 & 20; 10:38; 3:1; 7:15; 12:33b. Mark 8:29-38. Luke 24:50-51; 22:19; 20:1-10; 2:19. John 18:36; 3:16; 8:32; 19:30; 14:2-3 & 6; 20:1-10; 2:19; Romans 3:23; 5:20; 3:10; 1:16a; 12:1b; 3:25. 1 Corinthians 3:13; 15:5-6. 2 Corinthians 12:9. Ephesians 4:22-23; 3:6. Philippians 1:20. Colossians 3:9. 1 Thessalonians 4:16 & 17. 1 Timothy 2:5-6; 2 Timothy 1:7; 3:16. 1:13; 3:14-15; Hebrews 1:1; 2:4; 8:6; 12:24; 1 Peter 4:14a & 16a. 2 Peter 2:1a. James 1:8. Revelations 21:3 & 8; 5:20; 3:10; 20:15 & 19 & 20; Romans 10:3; Proverbs 8:13.

What is a Healthy Church? by Pastor Mark Denver

Delighting in God, by Dr. D. James Kennedy

Bible verses from new King James Version, New Geneva Study Bible and NIV.